It's a Sweet, Sweet World

50+ Dessert Recipes Including Ice Creams, Puddings, Cookies, and More

Kevin Jobson

Table of Contents

Introduction

Have you always wanted to make delicious desserts? Do you wish you could go to your next work party or family reunion with a homemade dessert in hand that everyone will rave about? Making fantastic desserts doesn't require a lot of time or even skill. All you need are a few great recipes with easy to follow instructions, and everyone will think you are an expert in the kitchen.

This recipe book will give you everything you need to create amazing desserts. Here, you will find a collection of recipes including everything from pies made entirely from scratch to shortcuts for making a boxed cake mix taste like it came from the best bakery in town. The ingredients are easy to find, and the instructions are easy to follow. Any recipe you choose from this book will provide you with a dish that will have everyone wanting more.

Chapter 1: Easy as Pie

Pie is delicious! Rather you eat it cold or warm, with Cool Whip or ice cream, there is nothing better than a nice slice of pie. You don't have to pick up a pie at the store or a baker. You can make your own from scratch, right down to the crust!

Traditional Pie Crust

Making your own pie crust might sound like something only bakery owners do, but it is a valuable skill. Being able to make your own crust means you can always bake a pie. Pie crust is made with ingredients that are probably always in your kitchen. This recipe is easy and delicious.

I know it seems like a daunting task, but this recipe makes it easy! There is no rolling out the dough trying to figure out if it's the right size or not. Simply press the dough into a pie pan with your fingers.

I recommend a deep dish 9-inch pie plate for all pie recipes.

Time: 20 minutes

Yield: 1 pie crust

Ingredients

- 1 ⅓ cups all-purpose flour
- ½ tsp salt
- ⅓ cup vegetable oil
- 2 tbsp ice water

Instructions

1. Preheat the oven to 475 °F. Butter pie dish.
2. In a medium mixing bowl add flour, salt and oil. Mix with a spoon until it forms a loose crumble.
3. Add ice water and continue to mix with spoon until dough forms large clumps
4. In the bowl, use your hands to shape dough into a ball.

5. Transfer dough to the buttered pie dish and use your
    fingers to press dough evenly into the dish and around
    the sides. Use a fork to poke holes in the bottom and
    around the sides of the dough. You can use the fork to
    press down gently around the top edge of the dish to
    create a pattern.
6. Bake pie dough for 10-12 minutes.

Graham Cracker Crust

Not all pie recipes call for a traditional crust. For example, cream pies will often go in a graham cracker crust. This is an easy task and requires only a few ingredients and no baking. This recipe can easily be altered to make a chocolate graham cracker crust by substituting the graham crackers for chocolate graham crackers.

Time: 40 minutes

Yield: 1 pie crust

Ingredients

- 1 ½ cups graham cracker crumbs (or crumbs from 12 crackers)
- ⅓ cup granulated sugar
- 6 tbsp unsalted butter (melted)

Instructions

1. In a bowl combine graham cracker crumbs, sugar, and butter. Mix with a fork until mixture resembles fine crumbs and sticks together.
2. Transfer mixture to a buttered pie plate.
3. Press mixture into pie plate working from the middle out and up the sides until the crust is an even thickness. This can be done easily by using the bottom of a measuring cup or a glass. This makes it easier to get around the edges of the pie plate.
4. Chill the crust in the refrigerator for 30 minutes or until you are ready to add filling.

Strawberry Pie

Strawberry pie is a crowd pleaser for all summer occasions. I recommend only using fresh strawberries for this recipe and serving with a dollop of whipped cream.

Time: 5 hours

Yield: 8 servings

Calories: 286

Fat: 7.6 g

Sodium: 171 mg

Carbohydrates: 55.8 g

Sugars: 44.5 g

Protein: 1.5 g

Ingredients

- 1 traditional pie crust
- 2 cups sliced strawberries
- 2 ½ tbsp cornstarch
- 1 ¼ cups granulated sugar
- 1 3 oz box strawberry gelatin
- Whipped cream for serving

Instructions

1. Prepare traditional pie crust according to instructions. Rinse and slice strawberries.
2. Once the pie crust has cooled, layer sliced strawberries in the crust.

3. In a saucepan, stir together sugar, cornstarch, and water.

4. Bring mixture to boil over medium heat stirring constantly with wire whisk. Mixture will bubble and thicken. When it is done it will be a thick, gel-like consistency.

5. Remove mixture from heat and stir in gelatin until completely dissolved.

6. Pour mixture over strawberries evenly.

7. Place pie in the refrigerator for approximately 4 hours until set.

8. Serve with whipped cream. Store covered in refrigerator for up to 4 days.

Cinnamon Pie

This pie is a great alternative to traditional pumpkin pie. It packs a punch of cinnamon, making it a great holiday dessert. This pie is best made the day before, giving the flavors plenty of time to marry together and make a delicious pie that everyone will beg you to make again.

Time: 50 minutes

Yield: 8 servings

Calories: 371

Fat: 24 g

Sodium: 421 mg

Carbohydrates: 35 g

Sugar: 27 g

Protein: 4 g

Ingredients

- 1 traditional pie crust
- 8 oz cream cheese, softened
- 1 ¼ cups heavy cream
- 1 cup brown sugar
- 2 large eggs and 1 egg yolk
- ¼ cup all-purpose flour
- 3 ½ tbsp ground cinnamon
- 2 tsp vanilla extract
- ½ tsp ground nutmeg

Instructions

1. Prepare traditional pie crust (do not pre-bake). Preheat the oven to 350 °F.
2. To a large mixing bowl, add cream cheese and brown sugar. Beat with hand mixer on high for about 5 minutes. Mixture will be fluffy. Scrape down the sides of the bowl, add eggs and egg yolk. Beat again with a hand mixer until combined.
3. Add cream to bowl and mix until combined. Then add flour, cinnamon, vanilla, and nutmeg. Mix again until the mixture is smooth.
4. Pour filling into pie crust. Bake for 35 minutes. When the pie is done, the center should jiggle slightly but not be liquid.
5. Allow the pie to cool completely, then cover and place in the refrigerator overnight. You will not want to wait, but believe me, it is worth it!
6. One hour before serving, take the pie out of the refrigerator. Serve dusted with powdered sugar or with a dollop of whipped cream.

Pumpkin Pie Cupcakes

If you love pumpkin pie, you're going to love these pumpkin pie cupcakes. These are great for a party because each person can have their own cupcake, and there's no need for a knife. These small, crustless pumpkin pies are best served cold with whipped cream. I suggest making them the day before you plan to serve them to allow the flavors to fully develop.

Time: 30 minutes

Yield: 12 cupcakes

Calories: 107

Fat: 2 g

Sodium: 96 mg

Carbohydrates: 20 g

Sugar: 14 g

Protein: 3 g

Ingredients

- 1 (15 oz) can of pure pumpkin puree
- ¾ cup granulated sugar
- 2 large eggs
- 1 tsp vanilla extract
- ¾ cup evaporated milk
- ⅔ cup all-purpose flour
- 2 tsp pumpkin pie spice
- ¼ tsp baking soda
- ¼ tsp baking powder

- ¼ tsp kosher salt (optional)
- Whipped cream for topping

Instructions

1. Preheat the oven to 350 °F. Place liners in a cupcake pan or spray wells with nonstick baking spray.
2. To a large bowl, add pumpkin puree, sugar, eggs, vanilla extract, and evaporated milk. Whisk until all ingredients are well incorporated and the mixture is smooth.
3. In a bowl combine flour, pumpkin pie spice, salt, baking soda, and baking powder with a whisk until evenly incorporated.
4. Pour dry ingredients into pumpkin mixture and mix with whisk until just combined.
5. Fill each cupcake well with ⅓ cup of batter. This is easily done using a cookie scoop for mess free transfer. Cupcake wells should be at least half full.
6. Bake for about 20 minutes. Cupcakes will be set when done. A knife or toothpick inserted in the middle of a cupcake will come out clean.
7. Transfer cupcakes to a plate and chill in the refrigerator for at least 30 minutes before serving. The flavor really develops when allowed to sit for several hours or overnight.
8. Serve cold with whipped cream.
9. Store leftovers in airtight container in refrigerator for 2-3 days

Key Lime Pie

This key lime pie is tart and delicious. It is perfect on a hot summer day or for anyone who prefers a less sweet dessert. For an extra special treat, freeze this pie. Allow to sit out for about 20 minutes before cutting and serving. This makes a frozen treat that everyone will enjoy.

Time: 30 minutes

Yield: 8 servings

Calories: 853

Fat: 52.9 g

Sodium: 556 mg

Carbohydrates: 82.5 g

Sugars: 72.2 g

Protein: 15.9 g

Ingredients

- 1 graham cracker crust recipe (prepared)
- 3 (8 oz) packages cream cheese, softened
- 2 (14 oz) cans sweetened condensed milk
- 12 tbsp lime juice (freshly squeezed or bottled will work)
- 1 tsp lime zest (optional)
- 8 oz container of Cool Whip (thawed)

Instructions

1. Place cream cheese into the bowl of a stand mixer or large mixing bowl. Beat on medium for 3-5 minutes until cream cheese is smooth.
2. To the same bowl, add sweetened condensed milk, lime juice, and lime zest. Mix until well incorporated.
3. Add Cool Whip to bowl, then with a rubber spatula gently fold the Cool Whip into the cream cheese mixture. This method allows for a fluffy, light filling. This should take 1-2 minutes to fully incorporate.
4. Transfer filling to pie crust, smoothing the filling as you go. All of the filling may not fit. That's okay, it makes for a great snack with a few graham crackers.
5. Refrigerate or freeze for three hours before serving.
6. Store covered in refrigerator for up to 3 days.

Peanut Butter Pie

This peanut butter pie is a personal favorite. It has a delicious chocolate graham cracker crust and a creamy, fluffy peanut butter filling that go perfectly together. This pie can be served chilled or frozen.

Time: 30 minutes

Yield: 8 servings

Calories: 596

Fat: 40.6 g

Sodium: 22 mg

Carbohydrates: 419 g

Sugar: 36.9 g

Protein: 11.8 g

Ingredients

- 1 chocolate graham cracker crust recipe (prepared)
- 1 cup heavy cream
- 1 (8 oz) pkg cream cheese, softened
- 1 cup creamy peanut butter
- 1 cup sugar
- 1 tsp vanilla extract
- 1 tbsp butter, softened
- Cool Whip and chocolate syrup for serving (optional)

Instructions

1. In a chilled bowl, beat heavy cream on high with a hand mixer until stiff peaks form (about 5 minutes). Place the bowl back in the refrigerator to keep chilled.
2. In a large mixing bowl, beat together cream cheese, peanut butter, sugar, vanilla, and butter until mixture is smooth and well combined.
3. Add heavy cream to peanut butter mixture and gently fold in using a rubber spatula. Mixture will be well combined, light, and fluffy.
4. Transfer mixture to pie crust and smooth out. Chill or freeze for three hours.
5. Serve with a dollop of Cool Whip and a drizzle of chocolate syrup. Store covered in the refrigerator for up to three days or covered in the freezer for up to one month.

Hoosier Pie

Hoosier pie is also known as sugar cream pie. Rumor has it, this pie originated in Indiana, the Hoosier State! This is a delicious vanilla custard pie with a dusting of cinnamon spice on top. The custard is cool and creamy, and the cinnamon gets a little crunchy in the oven. It's an amazing combination! This pie needs some time to chill in the refrigerator, so this is a great option to make the night before you intend to serve it. Store leftovers covered in the refrigerator for up to 3 days.

Time: 4 hour 50 minutes

Yield: 8 servings

Calories: 413

Fat: 24.3 g

Sodium: 223 mg

Carbohydrates: 49.2 g

Sugar: 36.6 g

Protein: 2 g

Ingredients

- 1 traditional pie crust
- 1 cup granulated sugar
- 4 tbsp cornstarch
- 2 cups heavy cream
- 4 tbsp salted butter
- 2 tsp vanilla extract (divided)
- ½ teaspoon ground cinnamon
- ½ tsp ground nutmeg

Instructions

1. Prepare pie crust and pre bake according to directions. Preheat the oven to 325 °F.
2. In a medium saucepan, add sugar, cornstarch, and heavy cream. Whisk together and cook over medium heat. Stir continuously with a wooden spoon, and bring mixture to a boil. Boil for about 2 minutes, continuing to stir, until mixture starts to thicken.
3. Remove the mixture from heat and add butter and vanilla. Stir to incorporate.
4. Transfer mixture to pie crust.
5. In a small bowl, combine cinnamon and nutmeg. Sprinkle this mixture evenly over the pie.
6. Bake for 25 minutes. The center of the pie will still be unset, but the pie will set as it cools.
7. Cool the pie completely at room temperature before moving the pie to the refrigerator for about 4 hours until chilled and set.

Chocolate Cream Pie

Chocolate pie is one of the best desserts ever. It's cool, creamy, and chocolatey. There are many ways to make chocolate pie, but this way is my favorite. This pie comes out dense but still fluffy and has just the right amount of chocolate flavor. Top this with Cool Whip and a few chocolate shavings for a beautiful presentation. This pie does need some time to chill in the refrigerator, so plan accordingly. Store leftovers covered in the refrigerator for 3 days.

Time: 4 hours 20 minutes

Yield: 8

Calories: 859

Fat: 34.7 g

Sodium: 322 mg

Carbohydrates: 79.6

Sugar: 60.1 g

Protein: 8.6 g

Ingredients

- 1 chocolate pie crust
- 3 ½ cups half and half
- ½ cup unsalted butter (cut into chunks)
- ⅔ cup granulated sugar
- ¼ cup cornstarch
- 9 egg yolks
- 9 oz semi-sweet chocolate (chopped)

- 2 oz bittersweet chocolate (chopped)
- 1 ½ tsp vanilla extract

Instructions

1. In a large saucepan, heat the half and half over medium heat until it starts to simmer. Stir continuously to prevent sticking or burning. Remove pan from heat.
2. In a large bowl that is heat proof, add sugar and cornstarch. Whisk to combine. Add the egg yolks to the sugar mixture and whisk until well combined and smooth (about 3 minutes).
3. Carefully, and in a thin stream, pour the half and half into the sugar/egg mixture while whisking constantly.
4. Once the mixture has been well combined, add it back to the saucepan. While whisking constantly, heat mixture over medium heat for about 4 minutes. The mixture will be very thick and have bubbles rising to the surface. Remove the pan from heat and add the butter and chocolate. Stir until well combined.
5. Pour the mixture through a sieve or fine strainer into a bowl, then transfer it to the pie crust.
6. Cover the pie, while it's still hot, with plastic wrap. The plastic wrap should be touching the pudding mixture. This will remove any film that forms on the pudding while it cools.
7. Chill the pie in the refrigerator for at least 4 hours before serving with a dollop of Cool Whip.

Chapter 2: Piece of Cake

Cakes aren't just for birthdays. A cake can be a delicious addition to any menu, and you can make it yourself. I know that sounds daunting, but cakes can be very simple to create. Many bakeries use doctored boxed cake mixes to make those delicious, beautiful cakes you see in their windows. Anyone can do that, and I'll tell you exactly how. Along with some unconventional cakes, I'll give you the tips and tricks to use a boxed cake mix you can find at any store to make a cake that everyone will swear you got from a bakery.

Doctored Up Boxed Cake Mix

The next two recipes will tell you how to take any boxed cake mix and make it taste like it came from an amazing bakery. No one will ever believe you made these cakes in your own kitchen! If you follow these instructions, you will have dense, moist, delicious cakes to serve friends and family (or you can keep them all for yourself). You can use these recipes on any boxed cake mix, but be sure you do not get a mix that has pudding in it. That will result in an incredibly thick batter that is hard to work with.

Vanilla Boxed Cake

This vanilla boxed cake mix can be made into a delicious bakery style cake by altering just a few ingredients. For a vanilla cake, I also recommend adding some almond extract to take the flavor to the next level. These instructions can be applied to any flavor cake mix that is 15.25 oz.

Time: 1 hour

Yield: 12 servings

Calories: 267

Fat: 15.2 g

Sodium: 265 mg

Carbohydrates: 29 g

Sugar: 20.3 g

Protein: 3.6 g

Ingredients

- 1 (15.25 oz) boxed vanilla cake mix (without pudding in the mix)
- 1 cup sour cream
- 2 large eggs
- ½ cup whole milk
- ⅓ cup vegetable or canola oil
- 1 tsp vanilla extract
- ½ tsp almond extract (optional)

Instructions

1. Preheat the oven to 325 °F. Spray the pan with nonstick baking spray or place cupcake liners in the pan.
2. Pour cake mix in a large mixing bowl. Add sour cream, eggs, milk, oil, vanilla extract, and almond extract (optional). Beat on medium with a hand mixer until all ingredients are incorporated.
3. Transfer mix to the pan you are using. The easiest way to fill cupcake liners is with a cookie scoop.
4. The back of the cake mix box will tell you approximately how long to bake, based on the type of pan you are using. When cakes are done, the top will be only slightly golden and a toothpick will come out with a few crumbs sticking to it. Place the cake pan on a cooling rack or carefully remove cupcakes and transfer to a cooling rack.
5. Allow cakes to cool completely before frosting. Store in an airtight container for up to 4 days.

Red Velvet Boxed Cake

Red velvet cake is something special. It has a unique chocolatey flavor that pairs perfectly with cream cheese frosting. It is a favorite at weddings and parties. You can make your own starting with a boxed cake mix and adding a few easy to find ingredients. Try storing this cake in the fridge and serving it cold for a sweet, cool treat.

Time: 1 hour

Yield: 16 servings

Calories: 289

Fat: 15 g

Sodium: 240 mg

Carbohydrates: 36.1 g

Sugar: 21 g

Protein: 4 g

Ingredients

- 1 (15.25 oz) boxed yellow cake mix
- 6 tbsp all-purpose flour
- ½ cup granulated sugar
- 5 tbsp unsweetened cocoa powder
- ½ cup vegetable oil
- 3 large eggs
- 2 tsp vanilla extract
- ½ cup milk
- 1 cup sour cream

- 2-3 tbsp red food coloring (depending on how vibrant you want the color to be)

Instructions

1. Preheat the oven to 325 °F. Grease and flour the pan you are using or place liners in a cupcake pan.
2. In a large mixing bowl combine cake mix, flour, sugar, and cocoa. Whisk ingredients together to combine.
3. Add vegetable oil, eggs, vanilla extract, milk, sour cream, and food coloring to the dry mixture. Mix on low speed to combine ingredients then increase to medium speed for about 2 minutes.
4. Bake according to instructions on the cake mix box based on the type of pan you are using. When cooked through a toothpick will come out clean or with very few crumbs sticking.
5. Transfer pan to cooling rack or remove cupcakes from pan and place on cooling rack. Once cakes are cooled completely, top with cream cheese frosting.

Buttercream Frosting

A good buttercream frosting recipe is a versatile addition to the list of things you know how to make from scratch. This recipe is easy and comes together in just a few minutes. This frosting is great for cakes, cupcakes, and cookies. The color of this frosting can be changed by adding food coloring. I suggest using gel coloring. Start with just a drop and add more until the desired color is achieved. Frosting can be refrigerated in an airtight container for up to 1 month.

Time: 10 minutes

Yield: 6 cups

Calories: 1074

Fat: 64 g

Sodium: 207 mg

Carbohydrates: 129 g

Sugar: 126 g

Protein: 1 g

Ingredients

- 2 cups unsalted butter (room temperature)
- 1 tbsp vanilla extract
- ½ tsp salt
- 7 cups powdered sugar
- 3 tbsp heavy cream or whole milk

Instructions

1. Place butter in a large mixing bowl and beat on medium speed for about 1 minute.
2. Add vanilla extract and salt, and beat on medium speed until combined.
3. Add powdered sugar one cup at a time mixing until incorporated after each cup.
4. Add 1 tbsp of heavy cream after every 2 cups of powdered sugar.
5. Mix on high until frosting is smooth and fluffy (about 5 minutes).
6. Add more heavy cream if frosting is too thick or more powdered sugar if frosting is too thin.

Cream Cheese Frosting

Cream cheese frosting is delicious no matter what you put it on. It's even delicious on its own. Seriously, after you make this frosting, eat a spoonful of it. You deserve it! This recipe is easy and quick. It is perfect for red velvet cake, banana cake, pumpkin cake or cookies, carrot cake—so many things! This frosting can be colored by adding food coloring. I suggest using gel coloring. Start with one drop and add more until desired color is reached. This frosting can be stored in the refrigerator in an airtight container for up to 2 weeks.

Time: 10 minutes

Yield: 7 cups

Calories: 425

Fat: 28.6

Sodium: 221 mg

Carbohydrates: 41 g

Sugar: 39.3 g

Protein: 3 g

Ingredients

- 1 ½ cups butter (room temperature)
- ½ cup cream cheese (room temperature)
- 7 cups powdered sugar
- 1 tsp salt
- 1 tbsp vanilla extract
- 2 tbsp heavy cream or whole milk

Instructions

1. In a large mixing bowl, beat butter and cream cheese on high speed until smooth (about 1 minute).
2. Add vanilla and salt, then beat on low speed until well incorporated (about 30 seconds).
3. Add powdered sugar to bowl one cup at a time, mixing to incorporate after each cup. Add cream one tbsp at a time as needed.
4. Mix on high speed until frosting is mixed well and smooth (about 5 minutes). Add more cream if frosting is too thick or more powdered sugar if frosting is too thin.

Banana Cake

Banana cake is a scrumptious way to use bananas before they go bad. The best bananas for this are very ripe and will have many brown spots on the peel. This cake cooks at a low temperature and then goes directly into the freezer. Before you start, clear out enough space for a 9x13 pan in your freezer, and line the area with a dish towel. This cake will be delicious topped with cream cheese frosting! This cake should be stored covered in the refrigerator for up to 4 days, but it never lasts that long at my house.

Time: 1 hour 20 minutes

Yield: 20 servings

Calories: 405

Fat: 10 g

Sodium: 290 mg

Carbohydrates: 60 g

Sugars: 43 g

Protein: 4 g

Ingredients

- 3 very ripe bananas
- 2 tsp lemon juice
- 3 cups all-purpose flour
- 1 ½ tsp baking soda
- ¼ tsp salt
- ¾ cup butter, softened

- 2 cups sugar
- 3 eggs
- 2 tsp vanilla extract
- 1 ½ cups buttermilk

Instructions

1. Preheat the oven to 275 °F (I told you it was low!). Spray a 9x13 pan with nonstick cooking spray.
2. Add bananas and lemon juice to a bowl. Mash together until there are no large clumps.
3. In a medium bowl, add flour, baking soda, and salt.
4. In a large bowl, mix butter and sugar on medium speed until well incorporated and fluffy (about 3-5 minutes). Add eggs and vanilla then beat on medium speed for about 1 minute.
5. Mix alternately flour mixture and buttermilk into butter and sugar. Start with flour mixture, then buttermilk, and repeat until all ingredients are mixed well.
6. Stir in bananas with a rubber spatula.
7. Pour the cake batter into the pan and bake for 1 hour 10 minutes. When done a knife inserted in the middle of the cake will come out clean or with very few crumbs sticking to it.
8. Immediately place the cake pan in your freezer for 45 minutes. If the cake is not completely cooled, allow it to cool the rest of the way on the counter. Once the cake is cooled completely, top with cream cheese frosting.

Lemon Poppyseed Bundt Cake

Lemon and poppyseeds are a classic combination. The tart lemon and the slightly sweet, floral hint of the poppyseeds are a perfect pair. Plus, the poppyseeds are so pretty speckled through the bright yellow lemon cake. This lemon poppyseed Bundt cake will be a crowd pleaser for sure. Everyone will be impressed with your ability to make such a delicate, classy confection. This one requires a bit more effort, but I promise it is worth it!

Time: 1 hour 30 minutes

Yield: 10 servings

Calories: 554

Fat: 22.3 g

Sodium: 162.8 mg

Carbohydrates: 82.9 g

Sugars: 51.7 g

Protein: 7.9 g

Ingredients for Cake

- 3 cups all-purpose flour
- 2 tsp baking powder
- ½ tsp salt
- 1 cup unsalted butter, softened
- 1 ½ cups sugar
- 4 large eggs (at room temperature)
- 1 cup whole milk
- 2 lemons (zested)
- 3 tbsp poppyseeds

Ingredients for Syrup

- ⅓ cup fresh lemon juice
- ½ cup sugar

Ingredients for Glaze

- 1 cup powdered sugar
- 4 tbsp lemon juice

Instructions for Cake

1. Preheat the oven to 350 °F and spray a Bundt pan with nonstick baking spray with flour. Place the pan in the refrigerator while preparing batter.
2. In a large mixing bowl cream butter, and add sugar slowly until ingredients are well incorporated. Continue to mix on medium speed about three minutes until the mixture is light and fluffy.
3. Add lemon zest and mix until incorporated. You will be able to see the yellow flecks throughout the mixture.
4. Add eggs to mixture one at a time while continuing to beat on medium speed.
5. In a medium bowl, whisk flour, salt, and baking powder together. Then add the dry mix to the butter mixture alternating with milk.
6. Add poppyseeds and stir with a rubber spatula. Be sure to scrape the sides and bottom of the bowl to incorporate the poppyseeds throughout the batter evenly.
7. Remove the pan from the refrigerator and pour batter into the pan. Bang pan lightly on the countertop a few times to bring air bubbles to the top. Pop the bubbles with a toothpick.

8. Bake for 1 hour. A toothpick inserted will come out clean when the cake is done. While the cake is baking, prepare the syrup and the glaze.

9. Place the cake pan on a cooling rack and brush the cake evenly with syrup. Then, let the cake cool for 15 minutes. Grab the cake pan with oven mitts and move pan around until you are certain the whole cake is loose and will come out of the pan. If needed, you can loosen stubborn areas with a butter knife.

10. Place the cake on a cooling rack over a piece of parchment paper.

11. Drizzle glaze evenly over the top of the cake, allowing the glaze to run down the sides.

Instructions for Syrup

1. Mix sugar and juice together in a bowl.

2. The sugar will not completely dissolve, so it is important to stir the mixture as you are brushing it on the cake.

Instructions for Glaze

1. In a bowl combine powdered sugar and half of the lemon juice. Stir well with fork or wire whisk.

2. Continue to add the remaining lemon juice by teaspoons until the mixture is smooth and the desired thickness. Powdered sugar will be dissolved well.

Soda Pop Cake

This cake is just plain fun! Kids will love it, and may even love helping you make it, because it has a fun mix of jello and soda that you pour over the cake. The best thing is you can make this any flavor you want. Just make sure your jello and soda are the same flavors, or flavors that complement one another. For this recipe, I will use strawberry flavors, but raspberry and orange are both delicious options, as well! This cake is best when it has plenty of time to chill, so consider making it the night before you want to serve it. Store any leftovers covered in the refrigerator for up to 3 days. With its fun flavors and creamy vanilla topping, this cake is perfect for a summertime celebration!

Time: 2 hours

Yield: 16 servings

Calories: 278.7

Fat: 12.2 g

Sodium: 350 mg

Carbohydrates: 39.7 g

Sugar: 31.2 g

Protein: 3.2 g

Ingredients

- 1 (18 oz) pkg white cake mix, plus ingredients to prepare cake as directed on the box
- 1 (3 oz) pkg strawberry jello mix
- 1 ½ cups water (boiling)

- 1 (12 oz) strawberry soda
- 1 (3 oz) pkg instant vanilla pudding mix
- 1 (8 oz) container Cool Whip (thawed)
- 1 cup milk

Instructions

1. Prepare the cake, according to the directions on the box.
2. When the cake has about 5 minutes left to bake, prepare the jello mix.
3. Boil water. While water is coming to boil, empty the jello packet into a bowl. Then, add the boiling water and the soda. Whisk for about 2 minutes until the jello powder is dissolved.
4. Remove cake from the oven, and immediately poke holes evenly all over the top of the cake. You can make small holes with a fork or larger holes with something round. Either way, the holes need to go nearly all the way through the cake.
5. Pour the jello mixture evenly over the cake. Place the cake in the refrigerator to cool (about one hour).
6. Make the topping now. To a large mixing bowl, add Cool Whip, pudding mix, and milk. Beat on a medium speed for about 2 minutes until the mixture is well combined.
7. Gently and evenly spread topping over the cake. Place back in the refrigerator for at least 30 minutes. Serve cake chilled.

Chapter 3: Ice Cream Dreams

There is nothing better than smooth, creamy, cold ice cream. There's so many flavors and kinds of ice cream, how could anyone ever choose just one? A few great recipes for homemade ice cream and ice cream-based desserts means you will not ever have to choose. Some of these ice cream recipes do not even require an ice cream maker, which means fewer dishes and more time to enjoy a delicious treat with your family and friends.

No Churn Cinnamon Ice Cream

This cinnamon ice cream is deliciously sweet with a tiny bit of cinnamon spice. This would pair well with warm apple pie, peach cobbler, or just on its own. There's no limit to the things that could be done with this easy ice cream recipe. Try adding cinnamon chips, toffee bits, or chocolate chips for an extra crunch. Starting with a cold bowl will aid in the whipping process of the cream. Place your bowl in the refrigerator or freezer for an hour before you start. Store covered in freezer for up to two weeks.

Time: 6 hour 5 minutes

Yield: 1 quart

Calories: 351

Fat: 20.6 g

Sodium: 99 mg

Carbohydrates: 37.4 g

Sugar: 36 g

Protein: 6.1 g

Ingredients

- 2 cups heavy cream
- 1 teaspoon ground cinnamon
- 1 (14 oz) can sweetened condensed milk

Instructions

1. In the bowl of a stand mixer or a large mixing bowl, whip the heavy cream until stiff peaks form when the mixer is turned off and raised out of the bowl. This will take at least 5 minutes.
2. Add cinnamon to the cream mixture then turn the mixer to low speed.
3. Slowly drizzle sweetened condensed milk into the bowl.
4. When mixture is well incorporated, transfer it to a freezer safe container with a lid. Freeze for 6 hours or until ice cream is set.

Homemade Vanilla Ice Cream

Vanilla ice cream is the perfect addition to any dessert. Having an easy, delicious recipe you can make at home means you can have ice cream anytime. Think ice cream sundae parties with your kids! With vanilla ice cream, anything can be a topping! This ice cream does not require an ice cream maker, in fact, it is made in a Ziploc bag. This recipe can easily be doubled or tripled to make a larger batch. This can be stored in an airtight container in the freezer for up to 2 weeks.

Time: 15 minutes

Yield: 2 servings

Calories: 460

Fat: 44 g

Sodium: 45 mg

Carbohydrates: 15 g

Sugars: 12 g

Protein: 2 g

Ingredients

- 1 cup heavy cream
- 2 tbsp sugar
- ½ tsp vanilla extract
- 4 cups ice
- ¼ cup kosher salt
- 1 gallon size freezer bag
- 1 quart size freezer bag
- Oven mitts or gloves

Instructions

1. Pour cream, sugar, and vanilla into the quart size freezer bag. Seal bag and mix well by shaking for about 1 minute.
2. Place ice and salt in a gallon size freezer bag. Seal bag and shake to combine.
3. Place the sealed quart size bag inside the gallon size bag. Seal gallon size bag.
4. Shake and turn the bag for about 10 minutes to mix the ice cream and allow it to freeze. Wear oven mitts or gloves to protect your hands from the ice.
5. Ice cream can be served immediately or placed in an airtight container in the freezer.

No Churn Chocolate Ice Cream

This recipe, much like the cinnamon ice cream recipe, does not require an ice cream maker. You can make this in a stand mixer or with a hand mixer. This recipe is simple, requires few ingredients and not a lot of your time. The best part, of course, is the delicious result! A great mix in for this would be peanut butter chips. What a classic combination! This can be stored in the freezer in an airtight container for up to two weeks.

Time: 6 hours 10 minutes

Yield: 6 servings

Calories: 502

Fat: 36 g

Sodium: 115 mg

Carbohydrates: 42 g

Sugars: 36 g

Protein: 8 g

Ingredients

- 2 cups heavy cream
- 1 (14 oz) can sweetened condensed milk
- ½ cup unsweetened cocoa powder

Instructions

1. In the bowl of a stand mixer or a large mixing bowl, pour heavy cream and whip on high speed until stiff peaks

form when the mixer is turned off and raised out of the bowl.

2. Add cocoa powder to the bowl and turn the mixer on low speed.
3. Slowly drizzle the sweetened condensed milk into the cream mixture. Continue mixing until well incorporated.
4. Transfer mixture to a freezer safe container with a lid. Freeze for 6 hours or until ice cream is set.

Ice Cream Sandwich Cake

That's right! Ice cream sandwich cake! This scrumptious dessert is made with store bought ice cream sandwiches. Does it get any easier than that? I don't think so. This ice cream dessert is perfect for the 4th of July or a summer birthday, but ice cream is perfect anytime. Don't be afraid to show up to Thanksgiving dinner with an ice cream cake. Someone will be thankful they don't have to eat pumpkin pie again. This cake can be stored covered in the freezer for about a week.

Time: 40 minutes

Yield: 16 servings

Calories: 342

Fat: 15 g

Sodium: 181 mg

Carbohydrates: 50 g

Sugar: 27 g

Protein: 5 g

Ingredients

- 24 ice cream sandwiches (unwrapped)
- 12 Oreo cookies (crushed)
- 1 jar hot fudge topping
- 1 (8 oz) tub Cool Whip (thawed)

Instructions

1. In a 9x13 pan, layer half of the ice cream sandwiches.
2. Spread half the container of Cool Whip on top of ice cream sandwiches.
3. Drizzle about half of the hot fudge topping over Cool Whip.
4. Top with half of the crushed Oreos.
5. Repeat steps 1-4.
6. Place the cake in the freezer for at least 30 minutes before serving. If making the cake ahead of time, cover the cake before placing it in the freezer.

Strawberry Shortcake Ice Cream Bars

These ice cream bars have a sweet, strawberry flavor and a delightful crunchy topping. This cool, creamy treat is sure to be a favorite for kids and adults alike. These are made with just a few simple ingredients and come together quickly. Everyone will be delighted with this yummy strawberry dessert. These can be stored covered in the freezer for up to one week.

Time: 2 hours 20 minutes

Yield: 9 servings

Calories: 619

Fat: 27.6 g

Sodium: 460 mg

Carbohydrates: 85.9 g

Sugars: 42.4 g

Protein: 4.7 g

Ingredients

- 35 golden Oreos
- 5 tablespoons unsalted butter (melted)
- ½ freeze dried strawberries
- 1 quart strawberry ice cream, softened

Instructions

1. Line a 9x9 pan with parchment paper.
2. Place cookies in a food processor and pulse until cookies are crushed into small crumbs (about 1 minute). Then

add the freeze-dried strawberries and pulse a few more times until the strawberries are broken into small pieces.

3. Add butter to the food processor. Pulse until the cookie mixture is moistened throughout. There should not be any butter visible in the mixture as it should all be absorbed by the cookies.
4. Pour half of the cookie mixture into the pan and use the bottom of a round measuring cup to press the mixture down firmly. Make sure it covers the entire bottom of the pan including the corners.
5. Now, using a rubber spatula, spread the strawberry ice cream evenly over the cookie crust.
6. Evenly cover the top of the ice cream with the remaining cookie mixture.
7. Cover the pan and place in the freezer for 2 hours before serving.

Peanut Buster Parfait Cake

Peanut Buster Parfaits have everything! Smooth, cool ice cream; sweet, salty peanut butter; crunchy peanuts and rich chocolate fudge. What a treat! You don't have to make a trip to your local ice cream shop to get this combination. You can make this at home, and even better, you can share it with your family and friends. This dessert can be made ahead and stored for up to 1 week in the freezer. For storing, cover the pan with an airtight lid or multiple layers of foil to prevent freezer burn.

Time: 3 hours 15 minutes

Yield: 24 pieces

Calories: 488

Fat: 25 g

Sodium: 190 mg

Carbohydrates: 55 g

Sugar: 45 g

Protein: 8 g

Ingredients

- 10 chocolate graham crackers
- 1 gallon vanilla ice cream, softened
- 14 oz peanut butter ice cream topping or 1 cup melted peanut butter
- 1 ½ cups shelled, dry roasted peanuts
- 7.5 oz chocolate Smucker's Magic Shell ice cream topping

Instructions

1. Line the bottom of a 9x13 dish with the chocolate graham crackers. You may need to break some crackers in half to make them fit and cover the entire bottom of the pan.
2. Smooth half of the softened ice cream over the graham crackers, then drizzle all of the peanut butter topping over the ice cream followed by half of the peanuts.
3. Next, carefully smooth the remaining ice cream into the pan and sprinkle the remaining peanuts on top.
4. Now, drizzle the Magic Shell topping over the peanuts and place dessert into the freezer for 3 hours.

Chocolate Ice Cream Layer Cake

Ice cream cake is delicious. It's perfect for a summer birthday or holiday. There's no need to buy an ice cream cake when it's so easy to make one at home. With just a few ingredients, this ice cream cake is ready to stick in the freezer to be enjoyed whenever it's time to celebrate. You can store leftovers in an airtight container in the freezer for up to 2 weeks.

Time: 1 hour 15 minutes

Yield: 12 servings

Calories:335

Fat: 15 g

Sodium: 235 mg

Carbohydrates: 48.6 g

Sugar: 33.2 g

Protein: 2.9 g

Ingredients

- 1 pkg chocolate Oreos
- ½ cup unsalted butter (melted)
- 1 quart chocolate ice cream, softened
- 1 quart ice cream flavor of your choice
- 1 ½ cups hot fudge ice cream topping
- 1 (12 oz) tub Cool Whip (thawed)

Instructions

1. Prepare the crust by adding cookies to a food processor. Use the pulse setting to turn the cookies into a fine crumb mixture. Add the melted butter to the cookie crumbs and stir until well combined.
2. Transfer this mixture to a 9x13 pan sprayed with a nonstick spray. Press the cookie mixture evenly throughout the bottom of the pan to create a crust. Pop this into the freezer to allow it to set.
3. While the crust is setting, place one ice cream flavor into a large bowl. Stir it well to smooth it out and make sure it is all softened. Spread the ice cream over the crust, smoothing it out evenly. Then, place the pan back in the freezer for about 30 minutes. During this time, allow the second ice cream flavor to thaw.
4. Add the second ice cream flavor to a large bowl and stir it to make sure it is smooth and evenly thawed. Carefully spread this ice cream on top of the first flavor. Put the pan back in the freezer for an additional 30 minutes.
5. Spread the hot fudge sauce on top of the ice cream and freeze for another 30 minutes.
6. Spread Cool Whip on top of the hot fudge layer, then add sprinkles if desired. Now, cover the dish with aluminum foil and freeze for at least 12 hours.
7. Before serving, allow the dish to sit out for about 10 minutes to thaw slightly. This will make the cutting process easier.

Ice Cream Toffee Pie

This ice cream pie is a crowd pleaser with its cold, creamy texture and bits of crunchy toffee. It comes together quickly, but needs several hours to freeze before serving, so plan accordingly. Leftovers from this pie can be stored covered in the freezer for up to 2 weeks.

Time: 37 minutes

Yield: 12 servings

Calories: 467

Fat: 28 g

Sodium: 241 mg

Carbohydrates: 51 g

Sugar: 44 g

Protein: 2 g

Ingredients for Sauce

- ¼ cup light brown sugar
- ¼ cup granulated sugar
- 2 ½ tbsp light corn syrup
- 2 tbsp unsalted butter
- ½ cup heavy cream

Ingredients for Ice Cream Pie

- 1 ½ cup heavy cream
- ½ cup powdered sugar
- ½ tsp vanilla extract

- 1 ½ cups whole milk
- 1 (3.5 oz) box instant vanilla pudding mix
- 8 oz toffee bits

instructions

1. Prepare the caramel sauce by adding to a medium saucepan: brown sugar, granulated sugar, and corn syrup. Bring mixture to a boil and use a candy thermometer to monitor the temperature. Boil until the mixture reaches 240 degrees.
2. Remove the pan from the heat and allow it to cool slightly (about 5 minutes). Stir in heavy cream.
3. Pour about ½ cup of this caramel sauce into the bottom of the crust.
4. Now, in a large mixing bowl, or the bowl of a stand mixer, add cream, powdered sugar, and vanilla extract. Beat until stiff peaks form (about 5 minutes).
5. Add pudding and milk to a bowl and whisk until well incorporated.
6. Add pudding to whipped cream mixture and fold in gently.
7. Now fold in the toffee bits (gently).
8. Transfer mixture to the pie crust, then sprinkle a few toffee bits on top.
9. Freeze the pie, covered, overnight.
10. Allow pie to sit out for about 15 minutes before slicing and serving. Top each serving with some of the remaining caramel sauce.

Chapter 4: Mix It All Together (Dump Cakes)

Dump cake doesn't sound like a particularly appetizing dish—I know. Trust me, these cakes are so good you will wonder why you haven't been making these your whole life! These cakes call for only a few simple ingredients thrown into a pan, pop it in the oven, and in no time your house smells amazing and you have a dessert that tastes like it took hours to make.

Pineapple Upside Down Dump Cake

This is the easiest way to make pineapple upside down cake. You do not need a bowl, or a spoon, or a mixer. You just need a 9x13 pan and a few simple ingredients. This dump cake is fruity and buttery. The cherries add a great texture and a delicious pop of flavor. This can be served at room temperature, chilled or, my favorite, warmed and topped with a scoop of vanilla ice cream. This can be stored covered in the refrigerator for up to 3 days.

Time: 30 minutes

Yield: 12 servings

Calories: 430

Fat: 16.7 g

Sodium: 373 mg

Carbohydrates: 67.8

Sugar: 44.7 g

Protein: 2.6 g

Ingredients

- 1 (15.25 oz) box of yellow cake mix (unprepared)
- 2 (20 oz) can of diced pineapple (drained)
- 1 (10 oz) jar of cherries (drained)
- ½ cup brown sugar
- 1 ½ sticks unsalted butter (sliced)

Instructions

1. Preheat the oven to 350 °F. Make sure juice is drained from pineapple and cherries.
2. Layer pineapple in the bottom of a 9x13 baking dish. Be sure to cover the entire bottom.
3. Next, spread cherries evenly over the pineapple, then sprinkle the brown sugar evenly on top.
4. Evenly spread the cake mix over the fruit and brown sugar, then place butter slices on top.
5. Bake for 25-35 minutes. When the cake is done, the top will be slightly browned and look set, and your house will smell like butter and brown sugar. Do not worry if it looks like some of the cake mix isn't combined. It will still be fine.
6. Allow the cake to cool for at least 20 minutes before serving.

Piña Colada Dump Cake

This dump cake has sweet pineapple and real coconut flakes. It is sure to make you think you're sitting on a beach somewhere with a frosty piña colada in hand. This is great served with ice cream or topped with whipped cream and cherries. With its fruity, tropical flavors, this dessert is perfect for a summertime get-together. Store any leftovers in an airtight container in the refrigerator for up to 3 days.

Time: 1 hour 10 minutes

Yield: 16 servings

Calories: 338

Fat: 18.7 g

Sodium: 300 mg

Carbohydrates: 39.7

Sugar: 26.8 g

Protein: 2.1 g

Ingredients

- 1 cup unsalted butter (melted)
- ⅓ cup spiced rum
- 1 (1 lb) packages frozen pineapple chunks
- 1 (15.25 oz) box yellow cake mix
- 2 cups sweetened coconut flakes

Instructions

1. Preheat the oven to 350 °F.

2. Evenly pour half of the melted butter in the bottom of a 9x13 baking dish

3. Stir the rum into the butter.

4. Now, add the pineapple chunks. They are cold and may cause the butter to begin to harden back up. This is okay. Just toss the pineapple around to coat the pieces with butter as well as possible.

5. Evenly distribute the dry cake mix over the pineapple chunks then sprinkle the coconut flakes on top.

6. Now drizzle the remaining butter over the cake mix. Transfer the pan to the oven.

7. Bake for about 1 hour. When it is done, the cake will appear golden and bubbly. It will continue to set as it cools.

Pumpkin Dump Cake

I know it's tradition to show up to Thanksgiving dinner with a nice pumpkin pie for everyone to share. This pumpkin dump cake is a unique spin on the classic dessert. You still get the pumpkin flavor everyone is looking for, but you also get a surprise texture from the cake mix and the crunch of the pecans. Plus, this is much easier to make! This is delicious served cold or at room temperature. I recommend making this the night before to allow the flavors to develop. Store covered in the refrigerator for up to 5 days.

Time: 1 hour 30 minutes

Yield: 12 servings

Calories: 279

Fat: 9 g

Sodium: 308 mg

Carbohydrates: 46 g

Sugar: 30 g

Protein: 5 g

Ingredients

- 1 (30 oz) can pumpkin puree
- 1 (12oz) can evaporated milk
- ⅔ cup brown sugar
- 3 large eggs
- 2 tsp pumpkin pie spice
- 1 tsp ground cinnamon

- 1 (15.25 oz) box yellow cake mix (unprepared)
- 1 stick unsalted butter (sliced)
- 1 cup chopped pecans (optional, but delicious)

Instructions

1. Preheat the oven to 350 °F. Spray a 9x13 pan with a nonstick cooking spray.
2. To the 9x13 pan add pumpkin, milk, sugar, eggs, pumpkin spice, cinnamon, and half of the cake mix. Mix well until all ingredients are combined.
3. Sprinkle the remaining half of the cake mix over the mixture. Top with pecans, then evenly place the sliced butter on top.
4. Bake for 50-60 minutes. When the cake is done a toothpick will come out clean. Cool in pan before serving.

S'mores Dump Cake

S'mores are the perfect treat on a crisp fall evening, sitting around a fire with a blanket. They are a classic autumn dessert! You can have s'mores anytime, though. They aren't just for fall evenings. S'mores can be a scrumptious addition to any party. Now, the weather doesn't always allow us to build a fire and toast marshmallows, but that doesn't mean you can't still have a s'more. This s'mores dump cake lets you have gooey marshmallow and chocolatey goodness anytime. This can be stored covered in the refrigerator for up to 3 days.

Time: 1 hour 30 minutes

Yield: 10 servings

Calories: 309

Fat: 16.2 g

Sodium: 257 mg

Carbohydrates: 37.3 g

Sugar: 23.2 g

Protein: 5 g

Ingredients

- 5 oz box of chocolate Cook & Serve pudding
- 3 cups whole milk
- 12 graham cracker squares
- 1 (15.25 oz) box devil's food cake mix
- ½ cup unsalted butter (sliced)
- 1 ½ cups semi-sweet chocolate chips (divided)

- 3 cups large marshmallows
- 8 oz Cool Whip

Instructions

1. In a saucepan, add pudding and whole milk. Whisk until well combined, then bring to a boil over medium heat. Stir constantly to prevent lumps or burning. Continue to cook until pudding thickens. Remove from heat to cool for 15 minutes. Preheat the oven to 350 °F.
2. Once the pudding has cooled, transfer it to a 9x13 baking dish. Then layer the graham crackers over the pudding.
3. Sprinkle one cup of chocolate chips on the graham crackers.
4. Evenly sprinkle cake mix over top. Then, place the butter slices evenly over the cake mix and bake for 25 minutes.
5. Remove the cake and lightly stir in any dry spots of cake mix.
6. Layer marshmallows on top, then sprinkle with remaining chocolate chips. Place back in the oven for 5-6 minutes. Marshmallows will be puffy and lightly browned when the cake is done.
7. Allow the cake to cool for about 20 minutes before serving.

Caramel Apple Dump Cake

This dump cake has apples, and it also has gooey caramel pieces. It's a great combination! This is so simple; you don't even need a mixing bowl. You can just layer everything in the pan and stick it in the oven. It will turn out perfectly. This is amazing served with a scoop of ice cream and a drizzle of caramel or chocolate syrup. Store leftovers in an airtight container in the refrigerator for up to 3 days.

Time: 55 minutes

Yield: 12 servings

Calories: 261

Fat: 13 g

Sodium: 415 mg

Carbohydrates: 36 g

Sugar: 19 g

Protein: 2 g

Ingredients

- 2 (20 oz) cans apple pie filling
- ¼ tsp allspice
- ¼ tsp cinnamon
- ½ of a 10.8 oz bag of chewy caramels (cut in half)
- 1 box yellow cake mix
- ¾ cup unsalted butter (sliced)

Instructions

1. Preheat the oven to 350 °F. Spray a 9x13 baking dish with a nonstick cooking spray (generously). In a small bowl, add allspice and cinnamon. Stir together with a fork.
2. To the baking dish, add both cans of apple pie filling. Sprinkle cinnamon mixture evenly over the apples. Stir gently with a rubber spatula to mix the spices in. Smooth mixture out evenly.
3. Sprinkle caramels evenly over the apples.
4. Evenly pour dry cake mix over the top.
5. Place cold butter pieces evenly around the pan on top of the cake mix.
6. Bake for about 45 minutes. When the top of the cake is golden and the sides are bubbly, it is done.
7. Serve warm.

Chocolate Cherry Dump Cake

Chocolate cake with a fruity cherry flavored burst in every bite! I'll have some of that. This dump cake is quick and easy with only 3 ingredients! This is perfect for black forest cake lovers, but it's much easier to make. This cake is perfect served warm with vanilla ice cream or a dollop of whipped cream. Store leftovers in an airtight container for up to 3 days.

Time: 50 minutes

Yield: 12 servings

Calories: 352

Fat: 12 g

Sodium: 318 mg

Carbohydrates: 60 g

Sugar: 19 g

Protein: 3 g

Ingredients

- 2 (20 oz) cans cherry pie filling
- 1 box dark chocolate cake mix (such as devil's food, unprepared)
- ¾ cup unsalted butter (melted)

Instructions

1. Preheat the oven to 350 °F. Spray a 9x13 pan with a nonstick cooking spray.

2. Dump both cans of pie filling in the baking dish.
3. Evenly spread dry cake mix over pie filling. Make sure the cake mix is spread evenly, but do not stir it.
4. Drizzle melted butter over the cake mix.
5. Bake for about 45 minutes. The top will be golden, and the sides will be bubbly when the cake is done.
6. Let the cake cool for a few minutes before serving.

Fresh Blueberry Dump Cake

This dump cake is a little different because it calls for fresh blueberries. It is definitely worth it though. The blueberries add a delicious burst of flavor. This dump cake is not only an amazing dessert, it is great for breakfast, as well. Take a few extra minutes to check the blueberries and make sure all the stems are removed. This is great with ice cream or by itself. Store leftovers in an airtight container in the refrigerator for up to 3 days.

Time: 1 hour

Yield: 6 servings

Calories: 438

Fat: 18 g

Sodium: 668 mg

Carbohydrates: 66 g

Sugar: 31 g

Protein: 4 g

Ingredients

- 4 cups of fresh blueberries (stems removed, rinsed)
- 1 tbsp lemon juice
- 1 (16 oz) box vanilla cake mix
- ½ cup melted butter

Instructions

1. Preheat the oven to 350 °F. Spray the inside of a round baking dish with a nonstick cooking spray.
2. Place blueberries in the baking dish.
3. Evenly spread the cake mix over the blueberries.
4. Drizzle melted butter over the cake mix.
5. Bake for about 35 minutes until the cake is golden.
6. Allow to cool about 5 minutes before serving.

Chapter 5: Want a Cookie?

Cookies are truly one of the greatest baked goods ever invented. There are thousands of kinds of cookies, so there is something for everyone. They are portable. You don't need a knife, a fork, or even a plate to enjoy a delicious cookie! They can be enjoyed warm or cooled, with icing or ice cream! No matter the occasion, you can't go wrong with cookies!

Perfectly Soft Chocolate Chip Cookies

Chocolate chip cookies are the most classic of cookies. Everyone loves a good chocolate chip cookie. You don't have to run to the bakery or even the grocery store to have soft, delicious chocolate chip cookies. You only need to run to your kitchen! These cookies are easy to make and will satisfy your sweet tooth for sure. This batter needs to be refrigerated for at least 1 hour before baking, so plan accordingly. These cookies can be stored in an airtight container for 4 days.

Time: 1 hour

Yield: 24 cookies

Calories: 191

Fat: 9.9 g

Sodium: 109 mg

Carbohydrates: 22.9 g

Sugar: 12.9 g

Protein: 2.7 g

Ingredients

- ¾ cups butter (room temperature)
- ¾ cup brown sugar
- ¼ cup sugar
- 2 eggs
- 2 tsp vanilla extract
- 2 ¼ cups all-purpose flour
- 1 tsp cornstarch

- 1 tsp baking soda
- ¼ tsp baking powder
- 1 ¾ cups mini chocolate chips

Instructions

1. Preheat the oven to 350 °F and line a baking sheet with parchment paper or baking mat.
2. In a large mixing bowl, add butter, sugar, and brown sugar. Mix on high speed until mixture is well combined, light, and fluffy.
3. Add eggs and vanilla to mixture and mix on medium until incorporated (about 1 minute).
4. In a medium mixing bowl, whisk together flour, cornstarch, baking soda, and baking powder.
5. Slowly add dry mix to butter mixture 1 cup at a time. Mix to incorporate between each cup. After adding the last of the dry mix, beat on medium speed for about 1 minute.
6. Stir in the mini chocolate chips with a spoon or rubber spatula
7. Use a medium cookie scoop to transfer dough to a baking sheet placing scoops about 2 inches apart.
8. Bake for 8-10 minutes. Cookies will not be set completely. Cool on baking sheet for one minute before transferring cookies to a cooling rack.
9. Molasses Ginger Cookies

These cookies taste like autumn! They are deliciously spicy and coated in sugar. They make your house smell like rich molasses, ginger, and cinnamon. These are soft, fluffy, and addicting. Seriously, try to eat just one. It's not possible! The key to these is taking them out of the oven before they are completely set. It keeps them soft and chewy. This dough needs to be refrigerated before baking, so plan accordingly. You can store these in an airtight container for up to 5 days.

Time: 25 minutes

Yield: 24 cookies

Calories: 149

Fat: 6 g

Sodium: 53 mg

Carbohydrates: 22 g

Sugar: 13 g

Protein: 1 g

Ingredients

- ¾ cup unsalted butter (room temperature)
- 1 cup brown sugar
- 1 egg
- ½ molasses
- 2 ¼ cups all-purpose flour
- 1 tsp ground ginger
- 1 tsp ground cinnamon
- 1 tsp baking soda
- ½ cup granulated sugar (for rolling)

Instructions

1. In a large mixing bowl or the bowl of a stand mixer, combine butter, and brown sugar. Beat on a high speed until mixture is light and fluffy.
2. Add molasses and egg to the mixture and mix on medium speed until well combined.
3. In a separate bowl, combine flour, ginger, cinnamon, and baking soda. Whisk to combine. Then add the dry

mixture to the butter mixture and mix by hand until combined.

4. Cover and refrigerate until the dough is firm (about three hours).
5. Preheat the oven to 350 °F and line a baking sheet with parchment paper or a nonstick baking mat.
6. Scoop dough with a medium cookie scoop or a spoon and roll into 1.5-inch balls.
7. Add granulated sugar to a shallow bowl or plate. Roll each dough ball in sugar. Place the dough balls on the baking sheet about 2 inches apart.
8. Bake for 7-9 minutes. Cookies will be golden, but the centers will not be set. Allow cookies to cool on the baking sheet before transferring to a cooling rack.
9. Repeat with remaining dough.

Huge Peanut Butter Cookies

Peanut butter cookies are the perfect combination of sweet and salty. They go great with a glass of milk or on their own. These cookies are so big that one will be enough for anyone. They have scrumptious peanut butter chips in the mix to add an extra burst of flavor! This dough requires chilling, so plan accordingly. You can store these cookies in an airtight container for about 3 days.

Time: 4 hours 20 minutes

Yield: 24 cookies

Calories: 140

Fat: 8.2 g

Sodium: 144 mg

Carbohydrates: 14.1 g

Sugar: 5.3 g

Protein: 3.4 g

Ingredients

- ½ cup butter (room temperature)
- ¾ cup peanut butter
- ¾ cup brown sugar
- ¼ cup granulated sugar
- 1 large egg
- 1 tsp vanilla extract
- 1 tablespoon milk
- ¼ tsp salt
- 1 tsp baking soda

- 2 cups flour
- 1 package peanut butter chips

Instructions

1. In a large mixing bowl, or the bowl of a stand mixer, add butter, peanut butter, and both sugars. Beat on high speed for about 3 minutes until mixture is light and fluffy.
2. Add egg, vanilla, milk, baking soda, and salt. Mix until all ingredients are incorporated.
3. Slowly add flour to the bowl while beating on slow speed. Mix until dough comes together.
4. Stir in the peanut butter chips, then scoop ¼ cup portions of dough onto a cookie sheet. This is just for chilling, so spacing doesn't matter. Chill for at least 4 hours before baking.
5. Preheat the oven to 350 °F. Line a cookie sheet with parchment paper or a nonstick baking mat. Evenly space cookie dough, about 2 inches apart, on the baking sheet.
6. Bake for 11-12 minutes. Bottoms of cookies will be slightly browned but the middle will not be set yet. This allows for a chewy cookie. Cool for 5 minutes on the baking sheet, then transfer to a cooling rack.

Double Chocolate Cookies

What can I say about double chocolate cookies? It's chocolate dough and chocolate chips! It's double the chocolate! These cookies are rich and chocolatey and gooey when they are warm. If you are a chocoholic, these are the cookies for you! This dough requires chilling, so plan accordingly. If you feel like switching it up, you can add white chocolate chips to the dough in place of the chocolate chips. These cookies can be stored in an airtight container for about 4 days.

Time: 30 minutes

Yield: 14 cookies

Calories: 244

Fat: 12 g

Sodium: 101 mg

Carbohydrates: 33 g

Sugar: 23 g

Protein: 3 g

Ingredients

- 1 cup all-purpose flour
- ⅔ cup cocoa powder
- ½ tsp baking soda
- ¼ tsp salt
- 1 stick (½ cup) + 2 tbsp unsalted butter
- ¾ cup brown sugar
- ¼ cup granulated sugar

- 1 large egg
- 1 ½ tsp vanilla extract
- 1 cup chocolate chips

Instructions

1. In a medium bowl, whisk together flour, cocoa, baking soda, and salt.
2. In a large mixing bowl or the bowl of a stand mixer, add butter and both sugars. Beat on medium speed about 5 minutes until mixture is light and fluffy.
3. Add egg and vanilla, then mix for about 30 seconds. Scrape down the sides of the bowl.
4. While mixing on low speed, add in dry ingredients and mix until well combined.
5. Stir in chocolate chips with a rubber spatula or spoon.
6. Cover bowl and refrigerate for at least 3 hours before baking.
7. Preheat the oven to 350 °F. Take the dough out of the refrigerator and allow it to sit for 15 minutes. Line a baking sheet with parchment paper or a nonstick baking mat.
8. Form 3 tablespoon portions of dough into balls and place about 3 inches apart on the baking sheet.
9. Bake the cookies for 11-13 minutes until the cookies are just set. Allow to cool on the baking sheet for about 10 minutes before transferring to a cooling rack.
10. Repeat with remaining dough.

Cool Whip Cookies

These cookies are soft, chewy, and coated in powdered sugar. They are easy to make with just a few ingredients. You can whip these up in a few minutes, and everyone will be delighted by the delicious flavor and gorgeous design created by rolling the dough in powdered sugar before baking. These cookies can be made using any flavor of cake mix, so the possibilities are endless! Store these in an airtight container for about 3 days, though I doubt they will last that long.

Time: 20 minutes

Yield: 20 cookies

Calories: 122

Fat: 1 g

Sodium: 197 mg

Carbohydrates: 26 g

Sugar: 15 g

Protein: 1 g

Ingredients

- 1 box of any flavor cake mix
- 2 cups Cool Whip (thawed)
- 1 large egg
- ½ cup powdered sugar (for rolling)

Instructions

1. Preheat the oven to 350 °F. Line a baking sheet with parchment paper or a nonstick baking mat.
2. In a medium bowl, add cake mix, Cool Whip, and egg. Stir until well incorporated.
3. Add powdered sugar to a small bowl.
4. Drop teaspoon portions of dough into powdered sugar and roll around until coated.
5. Place dough on the baking sheet. Bake for 8-10 minutes. Cookies will be set but only just starting to brown when they are done.
6. Move cookies to a cooling rack immediately to cool.
7. Repeat with remaining dough.

Chewy Sugar Cookies

Sugar cookies are classic and simple. The original cookie, you might say. These sugar cookies come out soft, chewy, and perfectly sweet. They are sure to be a hit at a party or family reunion. The key to these is to be careful not to over bake them. Between the chewy cookie and the slight crunch of the sugar coating, what's not to love? These can be stored in an airtight container for up to 5 days.

Time: 40 minutes

Yield: 30 cookies

Calories: 125

Fat: 6 g

Sodium: 79.3 mg

Carbohydrates: 16.7 g

Sugar: 8.4 g

Protein: 1.4 g

Ingredients

- 2 ¾ cups all-purpose flour
- 1 tsp baking soda
- ½ tsp baking powder
- 1 cup unsalted butter (room temperature)
- 1 cup + 2 tbsp granulated sugar
- 2 tbsp light brown sugar
- 1 large egg
- 2 tsp vanilla extract
- ¼ cup sugar (for rolling)

Instructions

1. Preheat the oven to 350 °F. Line a baking sheet with parchment paper or a nonstick baking mat.
2. In a medium bowl, whisk together flour, baking soda, baking powder, and salt.
3. In a large mixing bowl, or the bowl of a stand mixer, add butter and sugars. Beat on high speed until mixture is light and fluffy.
4. Add the egg and vanilla and mix until incorporated.
5. Add dry ingredients and mix until dough forms. The dough should be thick but not sticky. Use a rubber spatula to scrape the dough down and form a giant ball.
6. Scoop the dough with a medium cookie scoop or about 1 ½ tbsp portions. Drop into sugar for rolling and roll until the dough ball is coated. Transfer to a baking sheet and place dough balls about 2 inches apart.
7. Bake cookies for 7-8 minutes. The cookies should be soft but not doughy and will be just turning golden around the edges.
8. Allow cookies to cool on the baking sheet for about 5 minutes before transferring to a cooling rack.
9. Repeat with remaining dough.

Snickerdoodles

Snickerdoodles are just like sugar cookies, right? No, they are not. They are delectably spiced with cinnamon and fluffier than a sugar cookie. Make these for a party, a holiday, or just for yourself. Who needs a reason to whip up a batch of delicious snickerdoodles? This dough does require chilling, but it's a quick 15 minutes in the freezer. These can be stored in an airtight container for up to 5 days.

Time: 25 minutes

Yield: 35 cookies

Calories: 117

Fat: 5.6 g

Sodium: 77 mg

Carbohydrates: 15.9 g

Sugar: 8.2 g

Protein: 1.4 g

Ingredients

- 2 ¾ cups all-purpose flour
- 2 tsp baking powder
- ½ tsp salt
- 1 tsp cinnamon
- 1 cup unsalted butter (room temperature)
- 1 ¼ cups granulated sugar
- ¼ cup brown sugar
- 2 large eggs (room temperature)

- ½ tsp vanilla extract
- 3 tbsp granulated sugar (for rolling)
- 2 ½ tsp cinnamon (for rolling)

Instructions

1. In a medium bowl whisk together flour, baking powder, salt, and 1 tsp cinnamon.
2. In a large mixing bowl, or the bowl of a stand mixer, add butter, granulated sugar, and brown sugar. Beat on high speed until mixture is light and fluffy. Then add vanilla extract and eggs. Beat at medium speed for 30 seconds. Scrape down the bowl, then beat on medium for another 30 seconds.
3. While beating on a low speed, add the dry ingredients slowly. Mix until just combined.
4. Cover the bowl with plastic wrap and place it in the freezer for 15 minutes to set the dough.
5. While the dough is chilling, preheat the oven to 350 °F. Line a baking sheet with parchment paper or a nonstick baking mat. In a small bowl, combine sugar and cinnamon for rolling. Now you are all set to make some delicious cookies!
6. Scoop dough by 1 ½ tbsp portions and roll in cinnamon sugar mixture until coated. Place on a baking sheet about 2 inches apart. Bake for 8-10 minutes or until cookies look puffy and slightly brown on the bottom.
7. Cool for 1-2 minutes on a baking sheet before transferring to a cooling rack.
8. Repeat with remaining dough.

No Bake Cookies

No bake cookies are chocolatey, peanut buttery, chewy and so easy to make. These delicious treats are the favorite of many! They involve a few simple ingredients, and yes, there is cooking involved, but these beauties do not spend any time in the oven. Which makes it really easy for you to pick at them while waiting for them to cool (it's okay, everyone does it). These go great with a big glass of milk for dessert, a quick after school snack for the kids or even breakfast for yourself, they do have oats in them after all. These can be stored in an airtight container for about 3 days.

Time: 26 minutes

Yield: 24 cookies

Calories: 175

Fat: 9 g

Sodium: 90 mg

Carbohydrates: 23 g

Sugar: 18 g

Protein: 3 g

Ingredients

- ½ cup unsalted butter
- 2 cups granulated sugar
- ½ cup milk
- ¼ cup cocoa
- ¾ cup peanut butter

- 2 tsp vanilla extract
- 3 ½ cups quick cooking oats

Instructions

1. On a countertop or table, lay out sheets of parchment paper, enough for about 24 cookies. Measure out 3 ½ cups quick cooking oats and set aside. Measure out ¾ cup of peanut butter and set aside.
2. In a large pan, add butter, sugar, milk and cocoa powder.
3. Turn the burner to medium and mix ingredients as they melt and come together. Once the mixture starts to boil, time out one minute, then remove from heat.
4. Stir in vanilla and peanut butter until mixture is smooth.
5. Add oats and stir until combined. All oats will be covered with chocolate mixture.
6. Using a medium cookie scoop, scoop out mixture and drop onto parchment paper. Press down very lightly on each cookie with the back of the cookie scoop.
7. Cookies will need about 20 minutes to set, but good luck leaving them alone for that long.

Chapter 6: DIP-a-Dee-Doo

Dips aren't just for chips, ya know? Sure, chips and dip are delicious, but what about a sweet, fluffy dip for dessert? Dessert dips are great for parties because everyone can scoop some onto a plate and continue to mingle, or everyone can gather around the dip bowl to continue their conversations. Please, no double dipping! Everything from cookie dough dip to fruit salsa can make for an easy dessert that everyone will love!

Dunkaroo Dip

Remember Dunkaroos? They came in a little container with frosting and sprinkles and graham cracker sticks. They were delicious! The thought of Dunkaroos takes me back to my childhood. They aren't around anymore, but that doesn't mean you can't still enjoy a sweet blast from the past. Sure, kids will love this dip, but it's okay to make it just for yourself, too. The great thing about this recipe is that it only involves a few easy to find ingredients and very little of your time. Whip this up for a birthday party or even a gathering of your friends. Everyone will remember that classic treat and appreciate the memories it brings back. This dip can be stored in an airtight container in the refrigerator for 3 days.

Time: 35 minutes

Yield: 16 servings

Calories: 67

Fat: 4 g

Sodium: 32 mg

Carbohydrates: 6.6 g

Sugar: 5.8 g

Protein: 1.1

Ingredients

- 1 (18.9 oz) box funfetti cake mix
- 1 cup vanilla yogurt
- 8 oz Cool Whip (thawed)

- Rainbow sprinkles (optional)
- Animal crackers (for dipping)

Instructions

1. In a large bowl, add cake mix, yogurt, and Cool Whip. Stir gently with rubber spatula until well combined.
2. Add sprinkles and stir again to incorporate.
3. Chill in the refrigerator for at least 30 minutes before serving.
4. Serve with animal crackers.

Monster Cookie Dip

This dip is creamy and deliciously peanut buttery! It has everything your favorite monster cookies have, but you don't have to bake it. It's like eating cookie dough, which everyone wants to do, right? This dip has it all, peanut butter, oats, M&Ms, and chocolate chips! Your guests will be addicted to this dip—if you share it with them, that is! This is perfect served with pretzels for dipping. The dip can be stored in an airtight container in the refrigerator for up to 3 days.

Time: 45 minutes

Yield: 3 cups

Calories: 187

Fat: 10.9 g

Sodium: 98 mg

Carbohydrates: 20.7 g

Sugar: 18.4 g

Protein: 2.8 g

Ingredients

- 8 oz cream cheese, softened
- ½ cup unsalted butter, softened
- 1 cup creamy peanut butter
- 1 cup brown sugar
- 1 ½ cups powdered sugar
- ¼ tsp salt
- ½ cup quick cooking oats

- 1 cup M&Ms (mini work great for this)
- 1 cup milk chocolate chips

Instructions

1. In a large mixing bowl, or the bowl of a stand mixer, combine cream cheese, butter and peanut butter. Beat on a high speed until all ingredients are incorporated.
2. To the same bowl add the brown sugar, powdered sugar, salt, and oats. Beat on a high speed until mixture is light and fluffy (about 2 minutes).
3. Stir the candy and chocolate chips in by hand with a rubber spatula.
4. Transfer dip to a serving bowl and serve with pretzels.

Hot Chocolate Dip

This dip is perfect for a holiday party! Everyone loves a creamy, warm cup of hot chocolate. With this recipe, you can make the most delicious dip. It really does taste like a perfect cup of hot chocolate. Of course, you can serve this anytime, not just at holiday parties. That's the beauty of this cool dip. You can have amazing hot chocolate flavor even in the middle of the summer! Enjoy this with pretzels, cookies, or your favorite fruit. Store leftovers in an airtight container in the refrigerator for up to 3 days.

Time: 40 minutes

Yield: 2 cups

Calories: 500

Fat: 17.9 g

Sodium: 321 mg

Carbohydrates: 34.1 g

Sugar: 24.6 g

Protein: 48.7 g

Ingredients

- 1 (8 oz) pkg cream cheese, softened
- ½ cup plain Greek yogurt
- ½ cup marshmallow cream
- 1 cup powdered hot chocolate mix (Swiss Miss Dark Sensations works great for this)
- ¾ cup Cool Whip (thawed and divided)

- 1 tbsp mini marshmallows for sprinkling on top (optional)
- 1 tbsp crushed candy cane pieces for sprinkling on top (optional)

Instructions

1. In a large mixing bowl, beat cream cheese on medium speed until it is creamy. Then, add the yogurt, marshmallow cream, and hot chocolate mix. Beat mixture again on medium speed until it is fluffy (about 2 minutes).
2. With a rubber spatula, gently fold in ½ cup of Cool Whip until well incorporated.
3. Place mixture in the refrigerator for about 30 minutes so it can set just a bit.
4. Before serving, top with remaining Cool Whip, mini marshmallows, and candy cane pieces.
5. Serve with your favorite cookies, pretzels, or fruit (strawberries and apples work well).

Sugar Cookie Dip

This sugar cookie dip is lightly sweet and delicious with graham crackers or cookies! It can be whipped up in just a few minutes and it tastes just like the cookies grandma makes around the holidays. This is perfect for a holiday party, or any occasion, really. Just add festive sprinkles to the top to match the occasion, and it's the perfect sweet dish.

Time: 5 minutes

Yield: 8 servings

Calories: 251

Fat: 23.2 g

Sodium: 188 mg

Carbohydrates: 7.2 g

Sugar: 4.7 g

Protein:

Ingredients

- 2 cups dry sugar cookie mix (such as Betty Crocker)
- 2 (8 oz) pkgs cream cheese, softened
- 4 tbsp heavy cream
- Sprinkles for garnishing
- Graham crackers or cookies for dipping

Instructions

1. In a large mixing bowl, combine sugar cookie mix, cream cheese, and heavy cream. Beat on medium speed until mixture is light and fluffy (about 3 minutes).
2. Transfer to a serving bowl. This can be served immediately or chilled for about 30 minutes to set.
3. Before serving, top with festive sprinkles of choice. Serve with graham crackers and/or cookies.

Fruit Dip

There are many different kinds of fruit dip. A good fruit dip recipe can go a long way in creating a dish that everyone will love. They are easy and versatile, often going great with whatever fresh fruit is in season. I am going to share two amazing fruit dip recipes here. They offer different tastes and textures allowing you to meet whatever craving you have. The first recipe is an indulgence for sure. It has a thick, creamy texture and the perfect combination of sweet and savory flavors. Serve this with any type of fruit (strawberries are particularly delicious). Store this in an airtight container in the refrigerator for up to 5 days.

Time: 5 minutes

Yield: 8 servings

Calories: 190

Fat: 9.9 g

Sodium: 95 mg

Carbohydrates: 23.2 g

Sugar: 13.5 g

Protein: 2.1 g

Ingredients

- 1 (8 oz) pkg cream cheese, softened
- 1 (7 oz) jar marshmallow fluff
- 1 tsp vanilla extract

Instructions

1. In a medium mixing bowl, add cream cheese, marshmallow fluff and vanilla extract.
2. Beat on a medium speed until ingredients are well incorporated (about 3 minutes).
3. Transfer to a serving bowl if serving immediately, or cover and refrigerate until serving.
4. Serve with your favorite fruit.

Fruit Dip II

This fruit dip requires only two simple ingredients. This dip is light, fluffy, and slightly healthier than the recipe above. This is amazing served with apples, but any fruit will be delicious with this dip. Whip this up quickly when company shows up or make a big batch for a party. No matter when you serve this, it will be a hit, and no one will believe how easy it was to make. Store this in an airtight container in the refrigerator for up to 5 days.

Time: 5 minutes

Yield: 8 servings

Calories: 104

Fat: 7.2 g

Sodium: 18 mg

Carbohydrates: 8.9 g

Sugar: 8.3 g

Protein: 1 g

Ingredients

- 1 (8 oz) tub Cool Whip (thawed)
- 1 (6 oz) container of yogurt (any flavor)

Instructions

1. In a medium mixing bowl, add Cool Whip and yogurt.
2. Gently fold together with a rubber spatula until the ingredients are well incorporated. Mixture will be fluffy.

3. Serve immediately, or transfer the mixture to a covered
    bowl and refrigerate.

Cookie Dough Dip

We all want to just eat cookie dough straight out of the bowl, right? Well, with this cookie dough dip, you can do just that. This is creamy, buttery, and full of chocolate chips. This dip is great served with graham crackers, and would also be perfect for strawberries or apple slices. Kids will love this when, finally, you tell them it's okay to eat the cookie dough. Store leftovers in an airtight container for up to 3 days.

Time: 5 minutes

Yield: 4 servings

Calories: 549

Fat: 36.8

Sodium: 348 mg

Carbohydrates: 51.2 g

Sugar: 47.6 g

Protein: 5.2 g

Ingredients

- ½ cup unsalted butter, softened
- 1 (8 oz) pkg cream cheese, softened
- ½ cup brown sugar
- ¼ cup powdered sugar
- 1 tsp vanilla extract
- ¾ cups mini chocolate chips

Instructions

1. In a large mixing bowl, combine butter and cream cheese. Beat on a medium speed until the mixture is smooth and well combined (about 2 minutes).
2. Next, add brown sugar, powdered sugar, and vanilla extract. Beat on medium speed for another 2 minutes until mixture is well incorporated.
3. Now fold in the chocolate chips with a rubber spatula. You may want to reserve a small amount of the chocolate chips to sprinkle on top of the dip.
4. Transfer to a serving bowl and add the reserved chocolate chips on top.

Chapter 7: Salad for Dessert

I know what you're thinking. Salad is not a dessert. Sure, traditional lettuce salad would not make a great dessert, but there are many types of salad that are just sweet enough to be the perfect ending to a meal. Fruit salads, ambrosia, and fluffs are all types of salad that are great desserts. These dessert salads are wonderful in the summer, but can be enjoyed anytime. A great thing about most of these salads is that they can be served as a dessert or as a side dish at a summertime BBQ.

Raspberry Fluff Salad

This jello salad is cool, fluffy, and scrumptiously fruity. The frozen raspberries add a tartness and texture that will wake up your taste buds! This salad comes together quickly and can be made ahead or served immediately. When your guests get a taste of this, they will beg you for the recipe.

Time: 5 minutes

Yield: 12 servings

Calories: 122 g

Fat: 4 g

Sodium: 64 mg

Carbohydrates: 18 g

Sugar: 16 g

Protein: 5 g

Ingredients

- 1 (5 oz) box instant vanilla pudding
- 1 (32 oz) container of vanilla yogurt
- 1 (8 oz) container Cool Whip (thawed)
- 1 (12 oz) pkg frozen raspberries

Instructions

1. Sit raspberries out in a bowl to thaw for about 10 minutes.
2. In a large mixing bowl, add pudding mix and yogurt. Whisk together until well combined.

3. With a rubber spatula, fold in Cool Whip until well incorporated.
4. Now add the raspberries and fold in gently.
5. You can serve this immediately, or you can let it sit for a few minutes allowing the raspberries to thaw more and add flavor to the salad.

Ambrosia Salad

Ambrosia is a classic dessert salad. Your grandma made it, your mom made it, and now you can make it too! This salad is sweet and full of fruit and marshmallows. Whip this up for a family reunion and watch your relatives fawn over what a great cook you are. This salad is excellent to make the day before you plan to serve it. This allows the flavors to marry together. Store this salad in an airtight container for up to 3 days.

Time: 1 hour 15 minutes (at least)

Yield: 10 servings

Calories: 332

Fat: 14 g

Sodium: 71 mg

Carbohydrates: 37 g

Sugar: 37 g

Protein: 2 g

Ingredients

- ¾ cup heavy cream
- ¼ cup powdered sugar
- ½ tsp vanilla extract
- ½ cup sour cream
- 1 (11 oz) can mandarin oranges (drained well)
- 1 (10 oz) jar maraschino cherries (without stems)
- 1 (8 oz) can pineapple tidbits (drained well
- 1 ½ cups sweetened shredded coconut
- 4 cups mini marshmallows

Instructions

1. In a large mixing bowl that has been chilled in the refrigerator or freezer for an hour, add heavy cream, powdered sugar, and vanilla extract. Beat on a medium speed until mixture is the consistency of Cool Whip.
2. Stir in the sour cream by hand.
3. In a medium bowl, add oranges, cherries, pineapple, coconut, and marshmallows. Stir together. Then add this mixture to the Cool Whip mixture and gently fold in with a rubber spatula.
4. Cover bowl and chill for at least 1 hour, or up to 24 hours, before serving.

Orange Dream Salad

This salad tastes just like a cool dreamsicle making it a perfect treat on a hot summer day. The creamy, fluffy texture is a delightful treat without the melting mess of an ice cream bar. Be sure to plan ahead when making this salad as it does require time to chill before serving. This can be stored in an airtight container in the refrigerator for up to 3 days.

Time: 4 hours 20 minutes

Yield: 8 servings

Calories: 64

Fat: 3 g

Sodium: 28 mg

Carbohydrates: 7 g

Sugar: 7 g

Ingredients

- 1 (6 oz) pkg orange jello
- 2 (3 oz) pkgs Cook & Serve vanilla pudding
- 4 cups hot water
- 1 (8 oz) container Cool Whip
- 1 large can mandarin oranges (drained well)

Instructions

1. In a large saucepan, add jello mix, pudding mix, and water.
2. Bring mixture to a boil while stirring. Continue this until mixture turns clear.

3. Pour mixture into a large bowl and chill in the refrigerator for at least 4 hours (overnight is better).
4. Once cooled and set, add Cool Whip to the jello mixture and mix well. This can be done with a potato masher or a hand mixer on a low speed.
5. Gently stir in mandarin oranges.
6. Refrigerate the dish until ready to serve.

Pineapple Pretzel Fluff

This fluffy salad recipe is perfection! It has a cool, creamy texture with sweet, slightly tart bits of pineapple and crunchy, salty pretzel pieces. It's so good, and so easy to throw together, you can have this anytime. You don't need an excuse to make this delicious treat. You can make this dish up to 24 hours ahead of time, but if you do, keep the pretzel mixture in a Ziploc baggie until you are ready to serve the salad.

Time: 12 minutes

Yield: 10 servings

Calories: 372

Fat: 25.8 g

Sodium: 143 g

Carbohydrates: 36 g

Sugar: 33.5 g

Protein: 2.6 g

Ingredients

- 1 cup crushed pretzels
- ½ cup butter, melted
- 1 cup granulated sugar (divided)
- 1 (8 oz) pkg cream cheese, softened
- 1 (20 oz) can crushed pineapple (drained)
- 1 (12 oz) container Cool Whip (thawed)

Instructions

1. Preheat the oven to 400 °F. Line a baking sheet with parchment paper.
2. In a medium bowl, add pretzels, ½ cup sugar, and butter. Stir well, then pour the mixture onto the baking sheet. Make sure none of the mixture overlaps.
3. Bake the pretzel mixture for about 7 minutes until the pretzels are golden and the sugar and butter are sticking to the pretzels. Be careful not to overbake as this will burn quickly and easily. Allow mixture to cool on pan
4. In a large mixing bowl, combine cream cheese and remaining sugar. Beat on a medium speed until mixture is creamy (about 3 minutes).
5. Gently fold in the pineapple and Cool Whip.
6. Cover and chill in the refrigerator for at least 1 hour.
7. Before serving, add pretzel mixture and stir gently. You may want to reserve a small amount of pretzel mixture to sprinkle on top.

Vanilla Apple Grape Salad

This dessert salad is delightfully crunchy, filled with grapes and crisp apples. The tartness of the cranberries is perfect with the sweetness of the grapes and the vanilla dressing. This dish is lovely for a backyard BBQ in the Fall. It can be served as a dessert or a side dish. If there will be young children enjoying this delicious dish, consider taking the time to slice the grapes in half lengthwise as a safety precaution. Serve this dish immediately or chill until ready to serve. This can be stored in an airtight container in the refrigerator for up to 3 days.

Time: 30 minutes

Yield: 10 servings

Calories: 324

Fat: 17 g

Sodium: 96 mg

Carbohydrates: 42 g

Sugar: 36 g

Protein: 3 g

Ingredients

- 1 (8 oz) pkg cream cheese, softened
- 1 cup sour cream
- ½ cup brown sugar
- 1 tsp vanilla extract
- 1 lb seedless red grapes
- 1 lb seedless green grapes

- 3 red apples (cored and diced)
- ⅔ cup chopped pecans
- ½ cup dried cranberries

Instructions

1. In a medium bowl, add cream cheese, sour cream, brown sugar, and vanilla extract. Beat on a medium speed until mixture is well combined (about 2 minutes). Mixture will be smooth. Set aside.
2. In a large bowl, add grapes, apples, pecans, and cranberries. Toss to mix together.
3. Add dressing mixture to the fruit bowl and stir gently to cover the fruit evenly in the dressing.
4. Serve immediately or refrigerate until you are ready to serve.

Fruit Salad

This is unlike any fruit salad you have ever had before. The combination of tart fruits and a sweet dressing makes this absolutely delicious. You can add other fruits if you like, but the ones listed have been used in this family recipe for years. The dressing requires cooking and cooling, and the fruit salad needs time for the flavors to develop, so plan accordingly. This can be stored in an airtight container in the refrigerator for up to 3 days.

Time: 2 hours 30 minutes

Yield: 8 servings

Calories: 236

Fat: 1.6 g

Sodium: 22 mg

Carbohydrates: 57 g

Sugar: 45.6 g

Protein: 3.3 g

Ingredients

- ½ cup pineapple juice (saved from the pineapple you put in the salad)
- 2 eggs (beaten)
- ¾ cup sugar
- 2 tbsp flour
- 2 large apples (peeled, cored and diced)
- 4 kiwis (peeled and cut into small chunks)

- 1 large can mandarin oranges (packed in juice or water, drained well)
- 1 large can pineapple chunks (packed in 100% pineapple juice, drained well—reserve juice for dressing)
- 2 medium bananas (save for serving)

Instructions

1. In a medium saucepan, add pineapple juice, sugar, eggs, and flour over medium heat. Stir constantly to prevent burning. Cook mixture for about 5 minutes until it becomes thick. It will be a consistency similar to pudding.
2. Remove mixture from heat and allow to cool completely. For faster cooling, you can place the pan in the refrigerator on top of a towel.
3. While dressing is cooling, prepare the fruit.
4. Once the dressing has cooled, add apples and pineapple to a large bowl with a lid. Pour dressing over fruit and stir gently.
5. Next, add the oranges and the kiwi (these are more delicate and shouldn't be stirred as much). Gently fold the mixture together.
6. This salad can be served immediately, but it is best if allowed to chill in the refrigerator for at least 1 hour.
7. Immediately before serving, slice bananas and stir them in gently.

Fruit Salsa with Homemade Cinnamon Chips

Fruit salsa is a delicious way to sneak some fruit into your diet and still feel like you are indulging in something special. This salsa is full of fresh fruit and has a light dressing. It is perfect with homemade cinnamon chips (recipe included). This fruit salsa comes together quickly and is great for an afternoon snack or to take to a backyard BBQ. Store leftovers in an airtight container in the refrigerator for up to 3 days.

Time: 35 minutes

Yield: 2 cups

Calories: 357

Fat: 14 g

Sodium: 258 mg

Carbohydrates: 60 g

Sugar: 43 g

Protein: 3 g

Ingredients for Fruit Salsa

- 1 pint strawberries (rinsed and finely diced)
- 2 kiwis (peeled and finely diced)
- 1 granny smith apple (peeled and finely diced)
- 1 mango (peeled and finely diced)
- ¼ cup granulated sugar
- Juice from 1 lemon

Ingredients for Cinnamon Chips

- 6 flour tortillas
- ½ cup unsalted butter (melted)
- 1 cup granulated sugar
- 1 tbsp cinnamon

Instructions

1. Add all the diced fruit to a large bowl.
2. Pour the lemon juice over the fruit and then sprinkle with sugar. Stir gently to combine until fruit is evenly covered in sauce.
3. Cover the bowl and place it in the fridge for at least 30 minutes, allowing the juices to come out and the flavors to marry together
4. While the fruit is chilling, make the cinnamon chips.
5. Preheat the oven to 450 °F. In a small bowl, stir together sugar and cinnamon. Line a baking sheet with parchment paper.
6. Brush melted butter over each tortilla, turning to coat both sides. Cut the tortillas into wedges using a pizza cutter. Transfer wedges to a large Ziploc bag, add cinnamon sugar and shake until the chips are well coated.
7. Place tortillas, in a single layer, on the baking sheet and bake for about 7 minutes. Chips should be crispy when done.
8. Allow chips to cool to room temperature before serving with fruit salsa.

Chapter 8: Pudding

Everybody loves pudding! I'm not just talking about a box of pudding or a Snack Pack. Bread pudding, pudding pie, pudding cake! These are just some of the amazing pudding desserts that you can delight company with. Next time you need a delicious dessert for a crowd, whip up one of these puddings!

Homemade Vanilla Pudding

You could buy pudding at the store, sure. You could also just make this delicious, easy homemade vanilla pudding. It takes surprisingly few ingredients, and it's delicious! You can serve this warm or chilled, by itself or with a few graham crackers and a dollop of Cool Whip. Store this in an airtight container in the refrigerator for up to 3 days.

Time: 1 hour

Yield: 6 servings

Calories: 349

Fat: 18.9 g

Sodium: 166 mg

Carbohydrates: 41.6 g

Sugar: 33.8 g

Protein: 5.4 g

Ingredients

- 1 cup sugar
- 2 tbsp cornstarch
- 3 cups half and half
- 4 egg yolks (lightly beaten)
- 1 tbsp butter
- 2 tsp vanilla extract
- ¼ tsp salt

Instructions

1. In a medium saucepan, combine sugar and cornstarch by whisking for a few seconds. Now add half and half, stir and cook over medium heat. Whisk constantly to prevent sticking or burning.
2. Once mixture starts to boil, cook for two more minutes while whisking.
3. Remove pan from heat and carefully add 1 cup of mixture to a bowl with the egg yolks and stir. This will allow the eggs to temper in so they do not scramble when added to the hot pudding mixture. Slowly whisk the egg yolk mixture back into the pan.
4. Return to a gentle boil and cook for about two more minutes until mixture starts to thicken.
5. Remove pan from heat. Add butter, vanilla and salt. Whisk in until well incorporated.
6. Now, you may either transfer the pudding mixture into 6 small bowls or ramekins, or transfer it to one large bowl. Cover the pudding with plastic wrap and allow it to chill on the counter for 45 minutes. Pudding may be served warm, immediately, or after it has chilled for about 3 hours in the refrigerator.

Homemade Chocolate Pudding

Smooth, creamy, chocolatey pudding is almost sinfully delicious. It takes you back to your childhood when there was always a pudding cup in your lunch box. This homemade chocolate pudding will allow you to reminisce about your childhood, but you'll feel like an adult because you made it yourself! This is delicious, warm or chilled. I suggest serving it with a dollop of Cool Whip and maybe a few graham crackers. Try crushing them up for an added texture. Store this pudding in an airtight container in the refrigerator for up to 3 days.

Time: 40 minutes

Yield: 8 servings

Calories: 282

Fat: 9.5 g

Sodium: 107 mg

Carbohydrates: 48.9 g

Sugar: 39.7 g

Protein: 3.9 g

Ingredients

- 1 ⅓ cup sugar
- ⅔ cup cocoa
- ⅓ cup cornstarch
- 4 ½ cups milk
- 4 tbsp butter
- 1 tsp vanilla

Instructions

1. To a medium saucepan, add sugar, cocoa powder, salt, and cornstarch. Whisk together for a few seconds to combine. Add milk and whisk again to incorporate.
2. Cook over medium heat, whisking constantly, until mixture comes to a boil. Now, time out one minute of boiling.
3. Remove from heat and add butter and vanilla. Stir to incorporate.
4. You can transfer the mixture to 8 small bowls or ramekins, or transfer it to one large bowl. Allow to cool on the countertop for about 45 minutes. Stirring occasionally will prevent the pudding from forming a skin.
5. Serve warm or after chilling in the refrigerator for about 3 hours.

Easy Bread Pudding

Bread pudding is a rich, classic dessert that we often think will be difficult to make. You order it at a restaurant, and you think it must have taken hours. Only someone who knows their way around the kitchen could possibly make something so delectable. Well, guess what. You can make bread pudding. This recipe is easy and comes together quickly. The bread for this should be set out overnight or at least for a few hours to dry out. This helps the bread absorb the custard. Serve this warm with a delicious bourbon sauce and a scoop of vanilla ice cream. Store this covered in the refrigerator for up to 5 days.

Time: 1 hour

Yield: 16 servings

Calories: 124

Fat: 2.3 g

Sodium: 150 mg

Carbohydrates: 20.5 g

Sugar: 11.2 g

Protein: 3.9 g

Ingredients

- 8 cups bread (cubed)
- ½ cup raisins
- 4 tbsp bourbon (divided)
- 4 eggs
- 2 cups milk

- 2 tsp cinnamon (divided)
- ½ tsp nutmeg
- 1 cup + 2 tbsp sugar (divided)
- ¼ cup unsalted butter
- 3 tbsp heavy cream

Instructions

1. In a small bowl, combine raisins and 2 tbsp bourbon. Allow to sit for at least 30 minutes so the raisins soak up the bourbon. There will still be bourbon in the bowl, but the raisins will be visibly plumper.
2. Preheat the oven to 350 °F. Spray a 9x13 baking dish with nonstick baking spray.
3. In a large mixing bowl, combine milk, eggs, 1 tsp cinnamon, nutmeg, and ½ cup sugar.
4. Remove raisins from bourbon making sure to drain as much bourbon off as possible. Add the raisins to the mixing bowl and fold them in gently. Now, add the bread cubes and fold them into the mixture gently until coated evenly. Transfer this mixture to the baking dish.
5. In a small bowl, combine 2 tbsp of sugar and 1 tsp of cinnamon. Sprinkle this mixture over the bread pudding evenly.
6. Bake for 30-40 minutes. Bread pudding will be golden brown and puffy when it is done.
7. While bread pudding is baking, make the bourbon sauce.
8. In a medium saucepan, add 1/cup sugar, butter, heavy cream, and 2 tbsp bourbon.
9. Simmer over medium heat for about 5 minutes until mixture thickens. Stir continuously to prevent sticking or burning. Allow the mixture to cool for about 5 minutes. Pour over bread pudding to serve.

Sticky Toffee Pudding

Sticky toffee pudding is a classic English dessert, although in England it is called date pudding. Either way, it is deliciously sweet and gooey. The toffee sauce complements the flavor of the cake perfectly and adds the right amount of sweet and salty. Guests will be impressed you made this classic, delicious dish on your own! Serve this warm with a scoop of vanilla ice cream. This pudding can be stored covered in the refrigerator for up to 4 days.

Time: 1 hour 5 minutes

Yield: 14 servings

Calories: 265

Fat: 6 g

Sodium: 263 mg

Carbohydrates: 52 g

Sugar: 39 g

Protein: 3 g

Ingredients

- 1 ¼ cups pitted dates (roughly chopped)
- 1 tsp baking soda
- 1 cup boiling water
- 5 tablespoons unsalted butter (softened, divided)
- 2 cups brown sugar (divided)
- 2 large eggs
- 1 ½ all-purpose flour

- 2 tsp baking powder
- ¾ tsp salt
- ½ cup half and half
- ¾ tsp vanilla extract

Ingredients

1. Preheat the oven to 350 °F. Line an 8-inch springform pan with a parchment paper round and coat lightly with nonstick cooking spray.
2. Chop pitted dates into small pieces, or place them in a food processor and use the pulse setting until they look like large crumbs. Transfer dates to a small bowl and sprinkle them with baking soda.
3. In a large bowl, add 2 tbsp butter, 1 cup of brown sugar and eggs. Beat on a medium speed until combined (about 1 minute). With a rubber spatula, fold in the flour, baking powder, salt, and dates.
4. Transfer batter to the cake pan and bake for 40-50 minutes. When the cake is done, the center will spring back if pressed on lightly.
5. Cool the cake in the pan on a cooling rack for about 10 minutes before removing the cake from the pan.
6. While the cake is cooling, prepare the toffee sauce.
7. In a medium saucepan, combine half and half, 1 cup brown sugar, 3 tbsp butter, and the vanilla extract. Cook over a medium heat until the mixture thickens slightly. Stir frequently to prevent sticking or burning.
8. Allow sauce to cool for about 10 minutes before serving over the cake.

Amazing Banana Pudding

Banana pudding is the perfect dessert for a warm summer day, or a cold winter day, or any day, really! This recipe is a little different from the banana pudding your grandma has been making for years. This one uses instant pudding and a few other special ingredients to make it light and fluffy and full of delicious banana flavor! This does require some time to chill, so plan accordingly. It needs to chill for at least 4 hour hours, but if you can let it sit overnight, the flavors will develop, and the cookies will soften. This can be stored covered in the refrigerator for up to 4 days.

Time: 4 hours 15 minutes

Yield: 12 servings

Calories: 219

Fat: 11 g

Sodium: 89 mg

Carbohydrates: 29 g

Sugar: 19 g

Protein: 4 g

Ingredients

- 2 pkg Pepperidge Farm Chessmen cookies
- 6 medium bananas (sliced)
- 1 (8 oz) pkg cream cheese, softened
- 1 (14 oz) can sweetened condensed milk
- 1 (5 oz) box instant banana pudding

- 2 cups cold milk
- 1 (12 oz) tub Cool Whip (thawed)

Instructions

1. In a 9x13 baking pan, use 1 package of cookies to line the bottom. Top the cookies with sliced bananas.
2. In a large mixing bowl, add cream cheese and sweetened condensed milk. Beat on a medium speed until the mixture is smooth and seems well incorporated.
3. Add the milk and pudding mix to the cream cheese mixture. Beat on a medium speed for 2 minutes. Scrape down the sides and bottom of the bowl. Beat on medium for another 2 minutes.
4. Gently fold in the Cool Whip until well incorporated. You should not be able to see the white of the Cool Whip when the mixture is combined.
5. Pour the pudding mixture over the bananas in the baking dish. Spread evenly using a rubber spatula.
6. Top with the remaining package of cookies. Chill covered in the refrigerator for at least 4 hours.

Dirt Pudding

This unique take on dirt pudding is a family favorite. It uses vanilla pudding rather than chocolate, making it slightly less rich and enhancing the flavor of the cookies. It is fluffy, creamy, and absolutely addictive! This is best when allowed to chill for several hours or overnight before serving. Store leftovers (if you have any) covered in the refrigerator for up to 3 days.

Time: 3 hours

Yield: 12 servings

Calories: 435

Fat: 25.9 g

Sodium: 489 mg

Carbohydrates: 51.9 g

Sugar: 42 g

Protein: 5.3 g

Ingredients

- 1 pkg chocolate Oreos (crushed)
- 1 stick (½ cup) unsalted butter, softened
- 1 (8 oz) pkg cream cheese, softened
- 1 cup powdered sugar
- 3 cups cold milk
- 1 tsp vanilla extract
- 1 (8 oz) tub Cool Whip (thawed)
- 2 (3 oz) pkgs vanilla instant pudding mix

Instructions

1. Crush the cookies. The easiest way to do this is to place them into a plastic baggie, and smash them with a rolling pin. You can also put them in a food processor and pulse them until they are crumbs with very few big pieces remaining.
2. In a large mixing bowl, beat the cream cheese, butter, and powdered sugar until it is smooth (about 2 minutes). Now add the milk, vanilla extract, and pudding mixes to the cream cheese mixture. Beat on a medium speed until ingredients are well combined and pudding begins to thicken (about 3 minutes).
3. Fold in the Cool Whip until well incorporated. The mixture will be fluffy.
4. Cover the bottom of a 9x13 pan with some of the crushed cookies. Then pour in half the pudding mixture, spreading it evenly over the cookies. Add another layer of cookies (saving some to sprinkle on top). Then pour in the remaining pudding mixture. Sprinkle the last of the cookies over the top.
5. Chill in the refrigerator for at least 4 hours before serving. This can also be layered in a trifle dish or a large bowl.

Chapter 9: Crock-Pot Desserts

Sometimes you just don't have time to devote to dessert. You need something you can set and forget that will just be there when you are ready for it. Around the holidays or when you need something to take to a potluck, something you can just throw in a crock-pot that will be ready and warm when people decide to dig into it is perfect! These crock-pot desserts are great for any occasion.

Chocolate Lava Cake

This chocolate lava cake is warm, chocolatey, and gooey, all the best things! This recipe can be mixed up, thrown in a crock-pot, and served whenever you are ready. It is perfect with a scoop of vanilla ice cream. Now, you probably will not have any leftovers, but if you do, store them in an airtight container in the refrigerator for up to 3 days. Warm the leftovers before enjoying them.

Time: 2 hours 4 minutes

Yield: 12 servings

Calories: 294

Fat: 9 g

Sodium: 438 mg

Carbohydrates: 35 g

Sugar: 21 g

Protein: 4 g

Ingredients

- 1 (15.25 oz) box chocolate cake mix (unprepared)
- 1 (3.9 oz) box instant chocolate pudding (unprepared)
- 1 ¼ cups whole milk
- ½ cup vegetable oil
- 3 eggs
- ½ cup sour cream
- 1 tsp vanilla
- 1 (12 oz) bag semi-sweet chocolate chips

Instructions

1. Spray the inside of your crock-pot with a nonstick cooking spray, generously.
2. In a large mixing bowl, add cake mix, pudding mix, milk, oil, sour cream, vanilla, and eggs. Beat on a low speed for about one minute until ingredients are incorporated. Now increase mixing speed to medium and beat for an additional 3 minutes. Batter will be smooth when ready.
3. Transfer cake batter to crock-pot. Sprinkle the chocolate chips evenly on top. Do not stir them in.
4. Cover with a lid and set the crock-pot to low temperature. Cook for about 2 ½ hours until the top of the cake is set.
5. Serve warm with a scoop of vanilla ice cream.

Cranberry Walnut Bread Pudding

Bread pudding is delicious, but it can take some time to prepare. This crock-pot version comes together quickly, and you don't have to fuss over it in the oven. Just throw it in a crock-pot, and a few hours later...scrumptious, warm bread pudding. This is perfect for a holiday party or potluck. This bread pudding is delicious with ice cream or with the caramel sauce recipe included. Maybe even serve it with both! Store leftovers in an airtight container in the refrigerator for up to 3 days.

Time: 4 hours 20 minutes

Yield: 6 servings

Calories: 324

Fat: 13 g

Sodium: 250 mg

Carbohydrates: 45 g

Sugar: 26 mg

Protein: 9 g

Ingredients

- 2 ½ cups milk
- 3 large eggs
- ½ cup pure maple syrup
- 1 tsp vanilla extract
- ½ tsp ground cinnamon
- 5 cups bread cut into 1 inch pieces (dried out)
- 3 tbsp butter (divided)

- ½ cup walnuts (roughly chopped)
- ½ cup dried cranberries
- 1 can sweetened condensed milk
- 2 tbsp brown sugar

Instructions

1. Grease the crock-pot with 2 tbsps butter.
2. In a large mixing bowl, add milk, eggs, vanilla, and cinnamon. Whisk until well combined.
3. Add the bread to the milk mixture. Allow this mixture to sit for about 10 minutes so the bread can soak up some of the milk mixture.
4. Gently fold in the cranberries and walnuts. Transfer mixture to the crock-pot.
5. Set the crock-pot to the low setting and cook for about 4 hours. Pudding will be set when it is done.
6. When you are ready to serve the pudding, prepare the caramel sauce.
7. In a medium saucepan, combine sweetened condensed milk, brown sugar, and 1 tbsp butter. Cook over medium heat until mixture becomes bubbly and thickened (about 5 minutes). Stir constantly to prevent sticking or burning.
8. Serve the sauce warm over the bread pudding.

Monkey Bread

Monkey bread is a truly delicious treat. It's soft, gooey, buttery, and full of cinnamon flavor. It's a favorite of adults and children, alike. Try making this crock-pot monkey bread on Christmas morning so you can enjoy time with your family rather than running back to the kitchen every few minutes to check on breakfast. This is best served warm. Store leftovers in an airtight container in the refrigerator for about 2 days. Warm leftovers before eating.

Time: 2 hours 10 minutes

Yield: 6 servings

Calories: 310

Fat: 12 g

Sodium: 76 mg

Carbohydrates: 79 g

Sugar: 75 g

Protein: 2 g

Ingredients

- 2 tubes refrigerated biscuit dough (each biscuit cut into 6 pieces)
- 1 cup unsalted butter (melted)
- 1 cup brown sugar
- 1 tbsp ground cinnamon
- ½ cup granulated sugar

Instructions

1. In a small bowl, whisk together cinnamon and sugar. Spray the inside of the crock-pot with nonstick cooking spray.
2. Toss the biscuit pieces a few at a time in the cinnamon sugar mixture. Place the biscuits in the bottom of the crock-pot.
3. In a medium bowl, combine melted butter, brown sugar, and the remaining cinnamon sugar mixture that you tossed the biscuits in. Add mixture to the crock-pot, pouring over the biscuits.
4. Now, cover the crockpot with 2 layers of paper towel to absorb any moisture that will form. It is important that the paper towels are not touching the contents of the crock-pot.
5. Place the lid over paper towels and set the crock-pot to a high setting. Cook for about 1 ½ hours.

Heavenly Crock-Pot Dessert

This dessert is like a gooey brownie cookie cake. Yes, it's all those things! This calls for only 4 ingredients! It's that simple! Throw these things together in a crock-pot, and a few hours later you have a delicious, almost indescribable dessert. It's perfect with a scoop of vanilla ice cream. Add a drizzle of caramel sauce for an extra layer of flavor. Store leftovers in an airtight container in the refrigerator for up to 3 days. Reheat leftovers before eating.

Time: 3 hours 5 minutes

Yield: 10 servings

Calories: 129

Fat: 11.4 g

Sodium: 110 mg

Carbohydrates: 4.5 g

Sugar: 3 g

Protein: 2.5 g

Ingredients

- 1 (8 oz) box fudge brownie mix
- 1 (7,5 oz) pouch chocolate chip cookie mix
- ½ cup unsalted butter (melted, divided)
- 4 eggs (divided)

Instructions

1. Spray the inside of a crock-pot with nonstick cooking spray with flour.
2. In a large mixing bowl, add brownie mix, ¼ cup melted butter, and 2 eggs. Mix on a medium speed until well combined.
3. In another medium mixing bowl, add chocolate chip cookie mix, ¼ cup melted butter, and 2 eggs. Mix on a medium speed until well combined.
4. Now, drop spoonfuls of each batter in the crock-pot, alternating between the two kinds of batter and being sure to cover the bottom of the crock-pot.
5. Cover with the lid and set the crock-pot to a high setting. Cook for about 2 hours until the cake is set in the center.

Fried Apples

I know, I know. How do you fry apples in a crock-pot? Well, it's really simple, actually. As easy as shaking a bag and dumping it in a crock-pot. These fried apples are a versatile dish. They can be served over pancakes for breakfast, as a side dish, or with ice cream for a delicious, easy dessert. With just a few ingredients, and a few minutes of your time, this amazing dessert will cook itself! You can store leftovers in an airtight container in the refrigerator for up to 3 days.

Time: 2 hours 20 minutes

Yield: 8 servings

Calories: 305

Fat: 6.5 g

Sodium: 46 mg

Carbohydrates: 66.8 g

Sugar: 51.4 g

Protein: 1.2 g

Ingredients

- 1 (14 oz) bag of pre-sliced apples (Gala or Honey Crisp work well). You could also slice your own apples (about 5 large apples) for this recipe.
- 2 tbsp cornstarch
- ¼ cup granulated sugar
- ¼ cup brown sugar
- 1 tsp cinnamon

- 1 tsp vanilla extract
- ¼ cup unsalted butter (melted)
- 1 tbsp lemon juice

Instructions

1. Set your crock-pot to a high setting. In a medium bowl, combine the granulated sugar, brown sugar, and cinnamon. Stir together with a fork.
2. In a large Ziploc bag, add apples and cornstarch. Seal and shake around until apples are coated. Now, add cinnamon sugar mixture. Seal again and shake around until apples are coated well.
3. Pour the apples into the crock-pot. Then, top with melted butter, vanilla, and lemon juice. Stir mixture a few times.
4. Cook apples for about 2 hours. Apples will be soft, but not falling apart when they are done.

Crock-Pot Elvis

Elvis loved bananas and peanut butter. It's true! One of his favorite snacks was a peanut butter and banana sandwich. This scrumptious crock-pot cake gives you all the flavors of Elvis' favorite snack and more. Everyone is sure to love this rock 'n roll inspired dessert. This is delicious by itself, with a scoop of ice cream or topped with a dollop of whipped cream and a few fresh banana slices. Add a sprinkle of chocolate or peanut butter chips for an extra tasty bite. Store leftovers in an airtight container in the refrigerator for up to 3 days. Warm before eating.

Time: 3 hours 30 minutes

Yield: 12 servings

Calories: 459

Fat: 19.6 g

Sodium: 386 mg

Carbohydrates: 66.3 g

Sugar: 47.3 g

Protein: 6.7 g

Ingredients

- 1 (3.4 oz) pkg instant banana pudding mix (plus ingredients to prepare)
- 3 cups cold whole milk
- 1 pkg yellow cake mix
- ½ cup peanut butter
- 1 ½ cups peanut butter chips
- ½ cup chocolate chips

Instructions

1. Spray the inside of a crock-pot with a nonstick cooking spray.
2. In a medium mixing bowl, or in the bowl of a stand mixer, add pudding mix and milk. Beat on a medium speed for about 2 minutes until mixture is combined. Let this mixture stand for a few minutes until it begins to set.
3. While the pudding is setting up, prepare cake mix according to package directions. Add the peanut butter and mix well.
4. Pour pudding mixture in the crock-pot. Then, add the cake mix on top of the pudding.
5. Put the lid on the crock-pot and cook on a low setting for about 3 hours.
6. Evenly spread the chocolate chips and peanut butter chips on top, place the lid on and allow the cake to sit for about 15 minutes until the chips are partially melted.
7. Serve warm.

Rocky Road Cake

This crock-pot dessert has everything rocky road ice cream has, but it's warm and gooey. You can eat it with ice cream, that's fine, encouraged even. There's no wrong way to eat this amazing dish. Serve it to guests, and they will never believe it came out of a crock-pot. Store leftovers in an airtight container for up to 3 days.

Time: 4 hours

Yield: 8 servings

Calories: 586

Fat: 30.5 g

Sodium: 772 mg

Carbohydrates: 71.2 g

Sugar: 42.6 g

Protein: 11.2 g

Ingredients

- 1 (15.25 oz) pkg German chocolate cake mix (unprepared)
- 1 (3.9 oz) pkg instant chocolate pudding mix
- 3 eggs (lightly beaten)
- 1 cup (8 oz) sour cream
- ⅓ cup unsalted butter (melted)
- 1 tsp vanilla extract
- 3 ¼ cups milk (divided)
- 1 (3.4 oz) pkg chocolate cook and serve pudding mix (unprepared)

- 1 ½ cup mini marshmallows
- 1 cup semi-sweet chocolate chips
- ½ cup pecans (chopped)

Instructions

1. Spray the inside of a crock-pot with a nonstick cooking spray.
2. In a large mixing bowl, add dry cake mix, instant pudding mix, eggs, sour cream, melted butter, vanilla, and 1 ¼ cups milk. Beat on a medium speed for about 2 minutes until ingredients are combined.
3. Pour the batter into the crock-pot.
4. In a large saucepan over medium heat bring the remaining 2 cups of milk to a light simmer. Milk will be steaming but not boiling. Stir continuously to prevent sticking and burning.
5. Sprinkle dry cook and serve pudding mix over mixture in crock-pot. Then, pour the hot milk over the pudding mix.
6. Cook on a low setting for 3 ½ hours. Cake will not appear completely cooked. That's okay. The cake will set as it stands.
7. Remove the lid from the cake and let it sit for about 15 minutes. Now, add the marshmallows, chocolate chips, and pecans. Let the cake sit uncovered until the marshmallows are melted and gooey.
8. Serve warm.

Red Velvet Cake

Red velvet cake is one of the most loved desserts of all time. Traditionally, it takes a lot of time and effort to make from scratch. There are boxed mixes, and they are great. There's also this crock-pot recipe. Of course, this will not be anything like traditional red velvet cake, but it may be even better. You get to eat this while it's warm and gooey and topped with a delicious homemade cream cheese icing! You can store any leftover is an airtight container for up to 3 days.

Time: 3 hours 10 minutes

Yield: 8 servings

Calories: 697

Fat: 27 g

Sodium: 509 mg

Carbohydrates: 105 g

Sugar: 84 g

Protein: 11 g

Ingredients

- ¾ cups chocolate chips
- ¾ cups unsalted butter
- 2 cups granulated sugar
- 2 eggs
- 3 egg whites
- 1 ⅕ cups all-purpose flour

- .3 oz bottle red food coloring (optional, will enhance color)
- 2 tsp vanilla extract
- 2 tsp cocoa powder
- 1 ½ tsp baking powder
- 1 batch of cream cheese icing recipe (found in the "Cake" section)
- pecans (optional)

Instructions

1. Spray the inside of a crock-pot with a nonstick cooking spray.
2. In a microwave safe bowl, combine chocolate chips and butter. Microwave for 30 seconds at a time, stirring in between, until chips and butter are melted and well combined. After the mixture is completely melted, transfer to a large mixing bowl.
3. To the chocolate mixture, add the eggs and egg whites one at a time, whisk well between each one.
4. Now, add the flour, food coloring, vanilla extract, cocoa, and baking powder. Whisk mixture together for about 2 minutes until everything is incorporated.
5. Transfer mixture to the crock-pot and smooth out evenly.
6. Position a few paper towels under the lid to absorb moisture. Make sure they are not touching the food. Place lid on crock-pot and set to a low setting for about 2 and a half hours. When the cake is done, a toothpick will come out clean when poked into the middle.
7. While the cake is cooling, prepare the icing.
8. In a medium mixing bowl, beat cream cheese and butter on a medium speed until the mixture is well incorporated and smooth.

9. Add the powdered sugar and beat on a low speed (so you
    don't make a powdered sugar dust cloud) until the
    powdered sugar starts to dissolve into the cream cheese
    mixture. Add vanilla extract and beat on high speed for
    about 2 minutes.
10. Serve the cake with icing on top and a sprinkle of pecans.

Cinnamon Roll Apple Cobbler

Cinnamon rolls and warm apples. Sounds like a great combination! This cobbler calls for only 2 ingredients! It's that easy. This could be served for breakfast or dessert. There is really no wrong time to eat this. Store leftovers in an airtight container in the refrigerator for 2 days. Warm before eating.

Time: 3 hours and 5 minutes

Yield: 10 servings

Calories: 60

Fat: 1 g

Sodium: 29 mg

Carbohydrates: 16 g

Sugar: 8 g

Protein: 1 g

Ingredients

- 1 (21 oz) can apple pie filling
- 24 oz refrigerated cinnamon rolls

Instructions

1. Spray the inside of a crock-pot with a nonstick cooking spray.
2. Open cinnamon rolls (reserve icing for later) and cut each cinnamon roll into 4 pieces. Place on layer of cinnamon roll pieces in the bottom of the crockpot
3. Pour half of the apple pie filling over cinnamon rolls.

4. Repeat layers.

5. Set the crock-pot to a low setting and cook for about 2 and a half hours. When the mixture is done, the cinnamon rolls will be set.

6. Drizzle the icing from the cinnamon rolls over the top of the cobbler.

7. Allow the cobbler to cool for about 5 minutes, then serve warm.

Chapter 10: A Little Bit Healthier Now

Sometimes you want dessert, but maybe you are trying to lose a few pounds or you need to watch your sugar intake. Maybe you have a food allergy that often makes it hard for you to enjoy dessert items. Well, here is a collection of recipes that meet many different dietary requirements. These are all just as delicious as any other dessert! It's okay to treat yourself with these healthier takes on traditional desserts.

Greek Yogurt Lemon Cheesecake Bars

These delicious little bars are creamy, lemony and so easy to make. You will feel like you are indulging in scrumptious lemon cheesecake without all the calories! You can make this treat extra special by freezing the bars before enjoying them. Store leftovers in an airtight container in the refrigerator for up to 3 days or in the freezer for up to 2 weeks.

Time: 5 hours

Yield: 12 servings

Calories: 194

Fat: 9 g

Sodium: 82 mg

Carbohydrates: 21 g

Sugar: 13 g

Protein: 7 g

Ingredients (For Crust)

- 1 cup whole wheat flour
- 2 tbsp granulated sugar
- ¼ tbsp salt
- 1 tsp lemon zest
- 6 tbsp unsalted butter (cold, cubed)
- 1 tbsp cold milk

Ingredients (For Cheesecake)

- 3 cups Greek yogurt (full fat)
- ½ cup granulated sugar
- 1 tsp cornstarch
- 2 eggs
- 1 tbsp lemon zest
- ¼ cup lemon juice
- ½ tsp vanilla extract

Instructions

1. Preheat the oven to 350 °F. Spray an 8x8 baking dish with a nonstick cooking spray. Now, line the pan with parchment paper. You want a sheet of paper long enough that it hangs over on two sides. You will use this to lift the bars out later.
2. In a medium mixing bowl or the bowl of a stand mixer, add flour, sugar, salt, lemon zest, and butter cubes. Mix on low for about 1 minute to incorporate ingredients, then turn to a medium speed and mix for about 3 minutes. The mixture will be combined and the butter will be in small, pea sized, pieces.
3. Add milk to the bowl and mix on a medium speed until mixture forms a dough. It should stick together if you press it together.
4. Transfer this mixture to the baking dish and spread it around, pressing down with your fingers until there is an even layer in the pan.
5. Bake for 15 minutes. Cool on a wire rack.
6. While the crust is cooling, make the cheesecake filling.
7. Preheat the oven to 325 °F.
8. In a large mixing bowl, or the bowl of a stand mixer, add Greek yogurt, sugar, and cornstarch. Mix on a medium speed until mixture is well incorporated. Now, add eggs,

lemon zest, lemon juice, and vanilla extract. Mix on a medium speed for about 3 minutes until mixture is well combined and smooth.

9. Transfer mixture to the baking dish and smooth evenly over the crust. Bake for about 40 minutes. Cheesecake will be just set as it will continue to set as it cools.

10. Allow cheesecake to cool completely on a cooling rack. This will take about 2 hours. Then place it in the refrigerator to chill for about 3 hours before serving.

11. To serve, use the overhanging parchment paper to gently and carefully pull the bars up from the pan.

Flourless Peanut Butter Brownies

Peanut butter brownies! That's what this is. It's not kind of a brownie or sort of like a brownie. It is a brownie. You will never know there is no flour in these delicious, chocolatey little treats. These are so good; you will never eat a regular brownie again! Enjoy these chilled, room temperature or warmed slightly. They are amazing no matter how you eat them. You can store these in an airtight container for up to 4 days. If you live in a humid or very warm environment, I recommend storing these in the refrigerator.

Time: 30 minutes

Yield: 16 brownies

Calories: 169

Fat: 10.9 g

Sodium: 43.8 mg

Carbohydrates: 18.2 g

Sugar: 15 g

Protein: 2.6 g

Ingredients

- ¼ cup coconut oil
- ¼ cup peanut butter
- 1 1/4 cups chocolate chips (divided)
- ½ cup coconut sugar
- 2 tsp vanilla extract
- 2 eggs (lightly beaten)

- ¼ cup unsweetened cocoa powder
- 3 tbsp tapioca starch
- ¼ tsp salt

Instructions

1. Preheat the oven to 325 °F. Line an 8x8 baking dish with parchment paper then spray with a nonstick cooking spray. In a small bowl, add cocoa powder, tapioca starch, and salt.
2. In a microwave safe bowl, add coconut oil, peanut butter, and ¾ cup chocolate chips. Microwave in 30 second increments, stirring between each time, until mixture is smooth and melted.
3. Once the mixture is melted, add coconut sugar and vanilla extract. Stir until ingredients are well combined with the chocolate mixture.
4. Allow the mixture to cool for about 3 minutes, then add the eggs. Mix with a whisk until well combined.
5. Add all dry ingredients and stir with a rubber spatula until the mixture is well incorporated and smooth.
6. Add remaining chocolate chips and stir gently just until they are incorporated.
7. Transfer mixture to baking dish. Bake for about 20 minutes. They should not be completely set as they will continue to set as they cool.
8. Allow brownies to sit for at least 10 minutes before serving.

Banana Oat Chocolate Chip Cookies

These cookies come together quickly and with only a few ingredients you probably already have in your kitchen. They are full of oats and chocolate chips and held together with mashed up bananas making them a perfect, healthy treat. Your kids will love these, and they won't even know they are eating something that is good for them! These could be served for breakfast or dessert. Store leftovers in an airtight container for up to 3 days.

Time: 27 minutes

Yield: 16 cookies

Calories: 98

Fat: 2 g

Sodium: 79 mg

Carbohydrates: 17 g

Sugar: 5 g

Protein: 2 g

Ingredients

- 4 ripe bananas (mashed)
- 2 cups quick cooking oats
- 4 tsp cinnamon
- 2 tsp vanilla extract
- ½ tsp sea salt
- ½ cup dark chocolate chips

Instructions

1. Preheat the oven to 325 °F. Spray a cookie sheet with a nonstick spray. Mash bananas well with a fork.
2. To a medium mixing bowl, add bananas, oats, cinnamon, vanilla extract, and sea salt. Stir together for about 1 minute with a rubber spatula.
3. Add chocolate chips to the mixture and stir gently for about 30 seconds.
4. Drop 8 even spoonfuls of mixture onto the cookie sheet. Bake for about 20 minutes until cookies will no longer fall apart if moved.
5. Transfer to the cooling rack and allow to cool completely before serving.

Peanut Butter and Jelly Bars

Peanut butter and jelly is a timeless, classic snack. We all grew up on peanut butter and jelly sandwiches. If you still love peanut butter and jelly, but you want to avoid all the carbs and sugar, these bars are just the thing for you! They come together quickly and are ready as soon as they cool. They can be stored in an airtight container for up to 5 days.

Time: 50 minutes

Yield: 12 servings

Calories: 378

Fat: 18 g

Sodium: 154.8 mg

Carbohydrates: 28.1 g

Sugar: 17.4 g

Protein: 8 g

Ingredients

- ½ cup natural peanut butter
- ½ coconut oil (melted)
- ⅓ cup maple syrup
- 1 tsp vanilla extract
- 3 cups almond flour
- ½ tsp baking soda
- ¼ tsp salt
- ¾ cup jelly (your flavor of choice)
- ½ cup chopped peanuts

Instructions

1. Preheat the oven to 350 °F. Spray an 8x8 baking dish with a nonstick baking spray.
2. In a small mixing bowl, add peanut butter, coconut oil, maple syrup, and vanilla extract. Stir with a spoon until ingredients are mixed well.
3. In a large mixing bowl, add almond flour, baking soda, and salt. Whisk until incorporated. Add wet ingredients to dry ingredients and mix with a rubber spatula until ingredients are incorporated.
4. Spread ⅔ of the dough into the bottom of the baking dish.
5. Spread a layer of jelly over the dough and top with the remaining dough crumbled up. Sprinkle with peanuts.
6. Bake for about 30 minutes. The top will be golden when the bars are done.
7. Allow the bars to cool for about 30 minutes and then move them to the refrigerator. Let them cool for about an hour before serving. The longer they chill, the more developed the flavors will be.

Greek Yogurt Pumpkin Bread

This pumpkin bread is all you need this fall! It has all the flavors of autumn, the pumpkin, the spices, the nuttiness of the pecans. The secret, though, is that this pumpkin bread is made with Greek yogurt which means it has fewer calories and grams of fat! You don't need to feel guilty about enjoying this cool weather treat. It's great for dessert or breakfast! Store leftovers covered for up to 3 days.

Time: 1 hour 5 minutes

Yield: 1 loaf or about 10 servings

Calories: 194

Fat: 12.4 g

Sodium: 189 mg

Carbohydrates: 32.6 g

Sugar: 16.5 g

Protein: 4.9 g

Ingredients

- 1 cup pumpkin puree
- ½ cup vanilla Greek yogurt
- 1 large egg
- 1 tsp vanilla extract
- ⅓ cup coconut oil (measured when melted)
- ¾ cup brown sugar
- 1 tsp baking soda
- ¼ tsp sea salt

- 2 tsp ground cinnamon
- 1 tsp pumpkin pie spice
- ½ tsp nutmeg
- 1 cup all-purpose flour
- ½ cup oat flour (you can make this by grinding up oats in a food processor)
- ½ cup dark chocolate chips
- ½ cup chopped pecans

Instructions

- Preheat the oven to 350 °F. Spray the inside of a loaf pan with a nonstick baking spray.
1. In a large mixing bowl, or the bowl of a stand mixer, add pumpkin, Greek yogurt, egg, vanilla extract, melted coconut oil, and brown sugar. Beat on a low speed until mixture is well combined.
2. Now, in a different bowl, whisk together baking soda, salt, cinnamon, pumpkin pie spice, nutmeg, and both flours until combined.
3. Add dry ingredients to wet ingredients. Mix on a low speed for about 30 seconds until mixture is just combined. Now, stir in chocolate chips, pecans, or both if desired. Transfer mixture to the loaf pan.
4. Bake for about 50 minutes. A toothpick inserted in the middle of the loaf should come about clean. Allow bread to cool before removing from the pan and slicing.

Monster Cookie Energy Balls

Sometimes you just need a quick snack, something to grab on your way out the door or something to indulge in that feels like it's bad for you but really isn't. These cookie balls are perfect for all of those needs. They do not require baking, so they are very easy to make! They pack huge flavor into a bite sized snack. Full of gooey almond or peanut butter and chewy oats with little bits of chocolate or peanut butter pieces. These energy balls are the perfect treat! They are great for snacking, for breakfast on your way out the door, or for a dessert you can feel good about. These are best stored in an airtight container in the refrigerator and can be kept for up to 5 days.

Time: 40 minutes

Yield: 24 servings

Calories: 128

Fat: 8 g

Sodium: 56 mg

Carbohydrates: 19 g

Sugar: 12 g

Protein: 4 g

Ingredients

- 2 ½ cups old fashioned oats
- 1 cup almond butter (peanut butter will work too)
- ½ cup honey
- 1 tsp vanilla extract

- ½ cup mini chocolate chips
- ½ cup peanut butter chips or mini M&M candies

Instructions

1. In a medium bowl, add almond butter, honey, and vanilla extract. Stir together with a rubber spatula until ingredients are well combined.
2. Now, add oats and stir again until oats are coated and mixture is gooey.
3. Stir in chocolate chips and peanut butter chips or M&Ms.
4. Place the bowl in the refrigerator for about 30 minutes. This sets the mixture a little and makes it easier to roll into balls.
5. Once the mixture has set, scoop out by spoonfuls and roll by hand.
6. Store these in the refrigerator to prevent a gooey mess.

Conclusion

I hope you enjoyed this collection of recipes. These are truly delicious desserts, each made with love and patience. The best thing you can do with any of these dishes is to share it with your family or friends. Food is meant to bring people together. It is a part of our culture and helps shape who we grow to be. Desserts are an especially important part of how food reflects who we are. Everyone has a family favorite dessert, something only Grandma or your favorite aunt can make. You hope one day they will pass that recipe on to you so it can be part of your family forever.

Share these recipes with the people you love, and when you find that special one that everyone asks you to make again and again, make that your recipe. The one that you will be known for. When your children grow up, they will wait patiently for the day when you teach them how to make that one special dish, and your recipe will become their recipe.

References

Aimee. (2020, August 31). *Paula Deen's Banana Pudding Recipe*. Shugary Sweets. https://www.shugarysweets.com/banana-pudding/.

Allori, K. (2020, June 20). *Easy Blueberry Dump Cake*. Self-Proclaimed Foodie. https://selfproclaimedfoodie.com/blueberry-dump-cake/.

Aunt Lou. (2019, September 18). *Crock Pot Cinnamon Roll Apple Cobbler*. Recipes That Crock! https://www.recipesthatcrock.com/crock-pot-cinnamon-roll-apple-cobbler/.

The BEST Soft and Chewy Sugar Cookie Recipe. Life Love and Sugar. (2020, March 11). https://www.lifeloveandsugar.com/best-soft-and-chewy-sugar-cookies/.

Chelsea. (2020, January 27). *Healthy Pumpkin Bread {Moist & Delicious!}*. Chelsea's Messy Apron. https://www.chelseasmessyapron.com/the-best-healthy-greek-yogurt-pumpkin-bread/.

Collier, A. S., Author: & Collier, S. (2020, March 11). *Perfect Cinnamon Pie*. A Spicy Perspective. https://www.aspicyperspective.com/cinnamon-pie/.

Cool Whip Cookies {Easy 4 Ingredient Cookie Recipe with a Cake Mix}. Tastes of Lizzy T. (2019, August 29). https://www.tastesoflizzyt.com/lemon-cool-whip-cookies.

Couse, M. (2020, June 12). *Chocolate Chip Cookie Dough Dip*. Cookie Dough and Oven Mitt. https://www.cookiedoughandovenmitt.com/chocolate-chip-cookie-dough-dip/.

Crock Pot Red Velvet Brownies. https://www.recipesthatcrock.com/.

Easy and Simple Bread Pudding Recipe. pinerday.com. (2020, April 15). https://pinerday.com/easy-and-simple-bread-pudding-recipe/.

Fehr, A. (2020, June 2). *Molasses Cookies Recipe: soft and chewy! (VIDEO)*. The Recipe Rebel. https://www.thereciperebel.com/molasses-cookies-recipe/.

Fiona. (2020, January 8). *Soft Batch Double Chocolate Cookies*. Just so Tasty. https://www.justsotasty.com/soft-batch-double-chocolate-cookies/.

Fishkind, J. (2020, July 18). *Gooey Caramel Apple Dump Cake Recipe - Dump, Bake, Enjoy!* Princess Pinky Girl. https://princesspinkygirl.com/caramel-apple-dump-cake-recipe/.

Gooey Crock Pot Monkey Bread. (2020, September 3). https://centslessdeals.com/.

Heaven in a Crockpot. Pinterest. (2020, June 9). https://www.pinterest.com/pin/209558188891695630/.

Holly, Nilsson, A. H., Author, & Nilsson, H. (2020, July 7). *Homemade Chocolate Pudding {Classic Dessert}*. https://www.spendwithpennies.com/chocolate-pudding/.

HOMEMADE VANILLA PUDDING RECIPE. Butter with a Side of Bread. (2020, February 29). https://butterwithasideofbread.com/homemade-vanilla-pudding/.

Hot Chocolate Cheesecake Dip. Inside BruCrew Life. (2020, February 18). https://insidebrucrewlife.com/hot-chocolate-cheesecake-dip/.

Huff, L. (2019, October 2). *Piña Colada Dump Cake Recipe (Pineapple Dump Cake).* Snappy Gourmet. https://snappygourmet.com/pina-colada-dump-cake-spring-sweep-giveaway/.

Jessica. (2018, April 18). *Snickerdoodle Cookies.* Stuck On Sweet. https://www.stuckonsweet.com/snickerdoodle-cookies/.

Julia, A., Author, Julia, Mpho8, Teresa, Bower, H., ... Kj. (2018, May 25). *Creamy Vanilla Grape & Apple Salad.* Julia's Album. https://juliasalbum.com/creamy-vanilla-grape-apple-salad/.

Kat, & Caldwell, M. (2020, May 11). *Fruit Salsa with Cinnamon Chips.* Home. Made. Interest. https://www.homemadeinterest.com/fruit-salsa-with-cinnamon-chips-2/.

Kern, D. (2020, May 13). *XL Bakery Style Peanut Butter Cookies.* Crazy for Crust. https://www.crazyforcrust.com/xl-bakery-style-peanut-butter-cookies/.

Kiszka, L. (2020, August 8). *Dunkaroo Dip.* Stress Baking. https://stressbaking.com/dunkaroos-dip/.

Kristine. (2019, October 5). *Lemon Greek Yogurt Cheesecake Bars*. Kristine's Kitchen. https://kristineskitchenblog.com/lemon-greek-yogurt-cheesecake-bars/.

Laura. (2020, September 2). *Flourless Peanut Butter Brownies*. JoyFoodSunshine. https://joyfoodsunshine.com/flourless-chocolate-peanut-butter-brownies/.

Lori. (2019, December 29). *Mandarin Orange Jello Salad*. A Reinvented Mom. https://www.areinventedmom.com/orange-salad/.

Ludlum, B. (2020, August 4). *Banana Oatmeal Chocolate Chip Cookies: Healthy Chocolate Chip Cookies*. My Crazy Good Life. https://mycrazygoodlife.com/banana-oatmeal-chocolate-chip-cookies/.

Mahrlig, C. (2017, April 11). *Crock Pot Elvis Pudding Cake*. Spicy Southern Kitchen. https://spicysouthernkitchen.com/crock-pot-elvis-pudding-cake/.

Mahrlig, C. (2020, May 20). *Pineapple Pretzel Fluff*. Spicy Southern Kitchen. https://spicysouthernkitchen.com/pineapple-pretzel-fluff/.

Maria. (2020, September 3). *Best Chocolate Cream Pie*. Maria's Kitchen. https://www.mariasskitchen.com/.

Marie, A. (2019, November 26). *Caramel Toffee Ice Cream Pie*. Ashlee Marie - real fun with real food. https://ashleemarie.com/caramel-toffee-ice-cream-pie/.

Monster Cookie Dough Dip. Cookie Dough and Oven Mitt. https://www.cookiedoughandovenmitt.com/category/dips/.

Morrissey, E. (2020, July 21). *Healthy Peanut Butter and Jelly Bars*. Erin Lives Whole. https://www.erinliveswhole.com/healthy-peanut-butter-and-jelly-bars/.

Nora, Recipe by Nora from Savory Nothings, & by, R. (2020, May 23). *Slow Cooker Bread Pudding with Cranberries and Walnuts*. Savory Nothings. https://www.savorynothings.com/slow-cooker-cranberry-walnut-bread-pudding-with-caramel-sauce/.

Peanut Butter Cookies Recipe. Gimme Some Oven. (2019, December 2). https://www.gimmesomeoven.com/peanut-butter-cookies/.

pumpkin dump cake. Savory Nothings. (2020, June 4). https://www.savorynothings.com/.

RASPBERRY VANILLA JELLO SALAD. Butter with a Side of Bread. (2020, April 12). https://butterwithasideofbread.com/raspberry-vanilla-jello-salad/.

Rocky Road Chocolate Spoon Cake. The Farmwife Cooks. (2019, March 16). https://www.farmwifecooks.com/rocky-road-chocolate-spoon-cake/.

Sally. (2020, August 27). *Easy 5 Layer Ice Cream Cake*. Sally's Baking Addiction. https://sallysbakingaddiction.com/easy-5-layer-ice-cream-cake/.

Sam. (2019, August 19). *The Best Ambrosia Salad Recipe.* Sugar
Spun Run. https://sugarspunrun.com/best-ambrosia-
salad-recipe/.

Smores Dump Cake. Moms Recipe Collection. (2018, January
27). https://momsrecipecollection.com/smores-dump-
cake-dessert-recipe/.

Stacey aka the Soccer MomStacey is the creator of The Soccer
Mom Blog. (2020, June 19). *Slow Cooker Chocolate Lava
Pudding Cake.* The Soccer Mom Blog.
https://thesoccermomblog.com/slow-cooker-chocolate-
lava-cake/.

Sticky Toffee Pudding. Recipe Girl®. (2020, March 29).
https://www.recipegirl.com/sticky-toffee-pudding/.

Sugar Cookie Dough Dip. Yellow Bliss Road. (2020, September
2). https://www.yellowblissroad.com/sugar-cookie-dip/.

Sugar Cream Pie. House of Nash Eats. (1970, September 4).
https://houseofnasheats.com/.

All pictures sourced from pixabay.com and unsplash.com